The Patriot Act

Other titles in the Lucent Terrorism Library are:

America Under Attack: Primary Sources
America Under Attack: September 11, 2001
The History of Terrorism
Terrorists and Terrorist Groups

THE
LUCENT
TERRORISM
LIBRARY

The Patriot Act

James D. Torr

LUCENT BOOKS

An imprint of Thomson Gale, a part of The Thomson Corporation

THOMSON

™

GALE

Detroit • New York • San Francisco • San Diego • New Haven, Conn. • Waterville, Maine • London • Munich

LIBRARY OF CONGRESS CATALOGING-IN-PUBLICATION DATA

Torr, James D., 1974–
    The Patriot Act / by James D. Torr.
        p. cm. — (Lucent terrorism library)
    Includes bibliographical references and index.
    ISBN 1-59018-774-1 (hardcover : alk. paper)
1. United States. Uniting and Strengthening America by Providing Appropriate Tools Required to Intercept and Obstruct Terrorism (USA PATRIOT ACT) Act of 2001. 2. National security—Law and legislation—United States. 3. Terrorism—United States—Prevention. 4. Civil rights—United States. I. Title. II. Series.
    KF4850.T67 2005
    345.73'02—dc22

                                                              2005009043

Printed in the United States of America

Contents

Foreword

It was the bloodiest day in American history since the battle of Antietam during the Civil War—a day in which everything about the nation would change forever. People, when speaking of the country, would henceforth specify "before September 11" or "after September 11." It was as if, on that Tuesday morning, the borders had suddenly shifted to include Canada and Mexico, or as if the official language of the United States had changed. The difference between "before" and "after" was that pronounced.

That Tuesday morning, September 11, 2001, was the day that Americans began to learn firsthand about terrorism, as first one fuel-heavy commercial airliner, and then a second, hit New York's World Trade Towers—sending them thundering to the ground in a firestorm of smoke and ash. A third airliner was flown into a wall of the Pentagon in Washington, D.C., and a fourth was apparently wrestled away from terrorists before it could be steered into another building. By the time the explosions and collapses had stopped and the fires had been extinguished, more than three thousand Americans had died.

Film clips and photographs showed the horror of that day. Trade Center workers could be seen leaping to their deaths from seventy, eighty, ninety floors up rather than endure the 1,000-degree temperatures within the towers. New Yorkers who had thought they were going to work were caught on film desperately racing the other way to escape the wall of dust and debris that rolled down the streets of lower Manhattan. Photographs showed badly burned Pentagon secretaries and frustrated rescue workers. Later pictures would show huge fire engines buried under the rubble.

It was not the first time America had been the target of terrorists. The same World Trade Center had been targeted in 1993 by Islamic terrorists, but the results had been negligible. The worst of such acts on American soil came in 1995 at the hands of a home-grown terrorist whose hatred for the government led to the bombing of the federal building in Oklahoma City. The blast killed 168 people—19 of them children.

But the September 11 attacks were far different. It was terror on a frighteningly well-planned, larger scale, carried out by nineteen men from the Middle East whose hatred of the United States drove them to the most appalling suicide mission the world had ever witnessed. As one U.S. intelligence officer told a CNN reporter, "These guys turned airplanes into weapons of mass destruction, landmarks familiar to all of us into mass graves."

Some observers say that September 11 may always be remembered as the date that the people of the United States finally came face to face with terrorism. "You've been relatively sheltered from terrorism," says an Israeli terrorism expert. "You hear about it happening here in the Middle East, in Northern Ireland, places far away from you. Now Americans have joined the real world where this ugliness is almost a daily occurrence."

This "real world" presents a formidable challenge to the United States and other nations. It is a world in which there are no rules, where modern terrorism is war not waged on soldiers, but on innocent people— including children. Terrorism is meant to shatter people's hope, to create instability in their daily lives, to make them feel vulnerable and frightened. People who continue to feel unsafe will demand that their leaders make concessions—*do something*— so that terrorists will stop the attacks.

Many experts feel that terrorism against the United States is just beginning. "The tragedy is that other groups, having seen [the success of the September 11 attacks] will think: why not do something else?" says Richard Murphy, former ambassador to Syria and Saudi Arabia. "This is the beginning of their war. There is a mentality at work here that the West is not prepared to understand."

Because terrorism is abhorrent to the vast majority of the nations on the planet, President George W. Bush's declaration of war against terrorism was supported by many other world leaders. He reminded citizens that it would be a long war, and one not easily won. However, as many agree, there is no choice; if terrorism is allowed to continue unchecked the world will never be safe.

The volumes of the Lucent Terrorism Library help to explain the unexplainable events of September 11, 2001, as well as examine the history, personalities, and issues connected with the ensuing war on terror. Annotated bibliographies provide readers with ideas for further research. Fully documented primary and secondary source quotations enliven the text. Each book in this series provides students with a wealth of information as well as launching points for further study and discussion.

A Question of Balance

O n October 26, 2001—just six weeks after terrorists crashed jet-liners into the World Trade Center and the Pentagon—President George W. Bush signed into law the first major piece of legislation designed to help the government fight the war on terror. The Uniting and Strengthening America by Providing Appropriate Tools Required to Intercept and Obstruct Terrorism (USA PATRIOT) Act of 2001 is a large and complex piece of legislation. Its most important provisions deal with how the government investigates and prosecutes terrorists. The Patriot Act provides harsher penalties for terrorism and gives Federal Bureau of Investigation (FBI) agents increased authority to use wiretaps and to search suspects' homes, offices, and private records. While the U.S. Department of Justice (DOJ) and the Bush administration

argue that these provisions are crucial to preventing future terrorist acts, critics of the Patriot Act maintain that its search and surveillance powers undermine civil liberties, particularly individual privacy.

In many respects, the controversy over the Patriot Act is the latest chapter in a centuries-old debate about how to balance national security and individual freedom in times of crisis. However, discussion of the Patriot Act also centers on a very modern dilemma: How can the government use electronic surveillance to investigate terrorism, while also protecting the privacy of the average citizen?

Balancing Security and Liberty

As military analyst Roger Dean Golden explains, national security measures are often viewed as conflicting with individual liberty: "Freedom and security may be viewed on a continuum, with the assumption that, as one is increased, the other may decrease."[1] At one extreme, in a state of total anarchy, individuals have the freedom to do whatever they please. However, without any laws, individuals have little expectation of safety. At the other extreme, a totalitarian state is able to ensure the safety of its citizens by monitoring everything they do and eliminating anyone who poses a threat. But the people living in such a state have little freedom.

The goal of a democratic government is to find the best balance between security and liberty. This was the goal that the Founding Fathers sought to achieve

This illustration represents the government as an ominously large figure peering through a long telescope to monitor the computer activities of a private citizen.

Japanese Americans are interned in a California camp in this 1942 photo. During World War II, President Franklin D. Roosevelt ordered the internment of Japanese Americans after the bombing of Pearl Harbor in December 1941.

through the U.S. Constitution: The Preamble to the Constitution states that the document's purpose is not only to "insure domestic tranquility" and "provide for the common defence," but also to "secure the Blessings of Liberty." The first ten amendments to the Constitution—known as the Bill of Rights—enumerate some of the individual civil liberties that the U.S. government is bound to uphold. Among these are the First Amendment's guarantee of free speech, free assembly, and a free press, and the Fourth Amendment's protection against unreasonable searches and seizures and its guarantee of due process under the law. After the Civil War and the abolition of slavery, the Fourteenth Amendment was added. This amendment guarantees equal treatment under the law to all persons under U.S. jurisdiction.

"Over the course of America's history," writes Golden, "the body of law established by the U.S. Congress and interpreted by the courts has sought to maintain a proper balance between security and liberty."[2] In times of war and crisis, the law has sometimes shifted the balance in favor of security over freedom. For example, during World War I, Congress passed the Sedition Act, which made it a crime to criticize the government. This law sought to enhance security at the expense of the right to free speech. The president also has limited authority to affect the balance between security and liberty through executive orders. President Abraham Lincoln used this authority during the Civil War to imprison Southern sympathizers without trial (violating their right to due process), and President Franklin D. Roosevelt used his authority to order the internment of Japanese Americans during World War II (violating their right to equal treatment under the law).

While these measures were viewed as necessary for national security when they were enacted, most of these curtailments of civil liberties came to be viewed as mistakes once their respective crises had passed. For example, the Supreme Court struck down the Sedition Act as unconstitutional, and in 1988, President Ronald Reagan issued a formal apology for the World War II internment of Japanese Americans. At different points throughout American history, notes the American Civil Liberties Union (ACLU), "constitutional protections have taken a back seat to national security. But with the benefit of hindsight, Americans have regretted such assertions of new government power in times of crisis."[3]

A Shift Toward Greater Security

The Patriot Act represents another shift toward greater security, which organizations such as the ACLU have argued that Americans will come to regret. For example, arguing before Congress against passage of the Patriot Act, Senator Russ Feingold (D-WI) warned that

> there is no doubt that if we lived in a police state, it would be easier to catch terrorists. If we lived in a country where the police were allowed to search your home at any time for any reason; if we lived in a country where the government was allowed to open your mail, eavesdrop on your phone conversations, or intercept your e-mail communications . . . the government would probably discover and arrest more terrorists. But that would not be a country in which we would want to live.[4]

Similarly, the ACLU maintains that since the point of the war on terror is to defend freedom, the war cannot be won by curtailing freedom: "If we are intimidated to the point of restricting our freedoms and undermining our democracy," the organization proclaims, "the terrorists will have won a resounding victory indeed."[5]

Supporters of the Patriot Act deny that the U.S. government is repeating the mistakes of the past. In their view, pre–September 11 laws had gone too far putting privacy concerns over national security. They point to the case of militant extremist Sheik Omar Abdel Rahman, who was later convicted of conspiracy in the 1993 bombing of the World Trade Center. FBI agents suspected he was at the center of a terrorist cell operating in New York City, but with little hard evidence, they could not obtain a warrant to perform full surveillance. As a DOJ official explains,

> Here was a guy you knew had ties to a terrorist organization. . . . You knew he was meeting his followers in the mosque. The agents couldn't go in. They had to stop at the door because no crime had been committed yet. You look at that and say "You gotta be kidding me."[6]

A consensus among law enforcement agencies is that restrictions like these may have prevented federal investigators from uncovering, and possibly preventing, the September 11, 2001, plot. In this view, the Patriot Act's loosening of the restrictions on how federal investigators use surveillance does not curb civil liberties, but instead helps to protect both individual freedom and public safety. DOJ official Dan Collins argues, for example, that "the Act represents a measured, responsible, and constitutional approach to the threat of terrorist activities," and that it provides "tools to fight terrorism in a manner that preserves and enhances privacy."[7]

In the immediate aftermath of the September 11 attacks, the overwhelming majority in Congress felt that increased security measures were necessary. Representative Joseph Pitts (R-PA) expressed a typical view: "We're at war, and we need to give those who are fighting it the tools they need to win."[8] Notably, Feingold was the only senator to vote against passage of the Patriot Act; his dissent was criticized by many who believed a less-than-unanimous vote was unpatriotic.

Congress appears to have acted in accord with public opinion at the time. In the weeks after September 11, many polls showed that the American public supported antiterror measures, even those that restricted civil liberties. For example, in a February 2002 poll, 62 percent of respondents agreed that "Americans will have to accept new restrictions on their civil liberties if we are to win the war on terrorism."[9] Historian Jay Winik sums up this popular view that temporary restrictions on civil liberties are justified: "Our history demonstrates that wartime restrictions on civil liberties have neither been irrevocable nor have they curtailed our fundamental freedoms in times of peace." He writes, "Our democracy can, and has, outlived temporary restrictions and continued to thrive."[10]

Electronic Communications and Surveillance

To the extent that the war on terror is similar to past crises, both supporters and critics of the Patriot Act agree that history should be a guide. But a common theme in

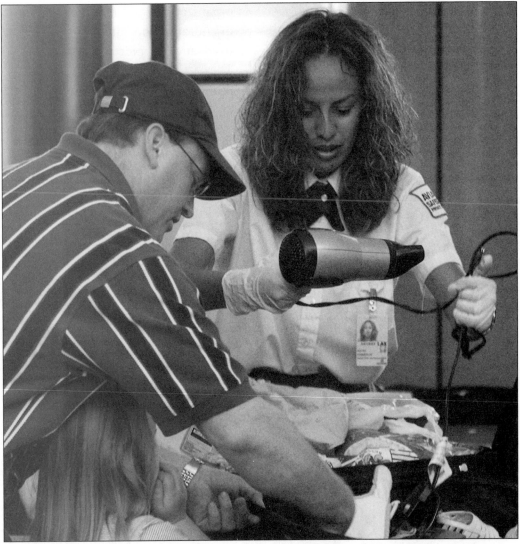

A security agent at the Los Angeles airport inspects a passenger's luggage. Following the September 11, 2001, terrorist attacks, airport security throughout the country was heightened.

the debate over the Patriot Act is that the current war on terror is different from past conflicts. On the one hand, September 11 showed that terrorists are more organized and capable of more destructive acts than was previously thought; they are also harder to identify than traditional enemies. On the other hand, in the course of trying to prevent terrorism, the government is authorized to collect more private information and more closely monitor more individuals than ever before.

Former attorney general John Ashcroft emphasized the extent of the terrorist threat when arguing before the House for passage of the Patriot Act in September 2001:

> The highly coordinated attacks of September 11th make it clear that terrorism is the activity of expertly organized, highly coordinated, and well financed organizations and networks. These organizations operate across borders to advance their ideological agendas. They benefit from the shelter and protection of like-minded regimes. They are undeterred by the threat of criminal sanctions, and they are willing to

President George W. Bush signs the Patriot Act into law on October 26, 2001. The act was designed to provide law enforcement with the tools needed to stop terrorist activity.

sacrifice the lives of their members in order to take the lives of innocent citizens of free nations.[11]

Terrorism is such a problem for law enforcement because terrorists have the element of surprise: It is likely that there will be little or no prior warning of when, where, or how the next attack will occur. Since guarding every potential target against terrorist attack is impossible, America's primary strategy in the war on terror is to prevent terrorism by identifying terrorists and learning of their plans before they are carried out. As Ashcroft put it, "We must prevent first—we must prosecute second."[12]

In order to fulfill this preventative role, the government must spy on suspected terrorists. In addition to having law enforcement agents actually follow suspected terrorists, eavesdrop on their face-to-face conversations, and perform physical searches of their homes or headquarters, investigators often also need to monitor their communications. Journalist Heather Mac-Donald emphasizes that "communications technology is essential to an enemy that has no geographical locus, and whose combatants have mastered the Internet and every form of modern communications, along with methods to defeat surveillance, such as using and discarding multiple cell phones and communicating from Internet cafes." Therefore, some of the most important provisions of the Patriot Act increase investigators' authority to use phone wiretaps and monitor Internet and e-mail use. Mac-Donald argues that these measures "simply

brought the law into the twenty-first century."[13]

However, from a civil liberties perspective, some of the most troubling aspects of the Patriot Act are the broad nature of these surveillance powers and the danger that they might be abused. Jay Stanley and Barry Steinhardt of the ACLU describe the Patriot Act as "an overnight revision of the nation's surveillance laws that vastly expanded the government's authority to spy on its own citizens."[14] Critics such as Stanley and Steinhardt often invoke George Orwell's novel *1984*, which depicts a dark future in which a totalitarian government called "Big Brother" monitors the movements, actions, and even the thoughts of its citizens. While the measures in the Patriot Act are not nearly so threatening, Stanley and Steinhardt warn that they may be a first step toward a broader "surveillance society": "If we do not take steps to control and regulate surveillance to bring it into conformity with our values, we will find ourselves being tracked, analyzed, profiled, and flagged in our daily lives to a degree we can scarcely imagine today."[15]

New Difficulties in Maintaining a Traditional Balance

The controversy over the Patriot Act is the latest chapter in the historic debate over how to balance security and civil liberties during wartime. But the war on terror also adds a new dimension to that debate. The threat of terrorism may be more of a danger to the United States than anything it has faced before, and therefore the measures used to combat this threat may need to be evaluated differently than Americans are used to doing. As political scientist Donald F. Kettl explains, "With the nation tiptoeing into new problems it had never faced before, it needed to devise new and untested policies to solve uncertain issues."[16] Homeland security measures raise the difficult question of how to balance the privacy of millions of Americans against the need to identify and investigate potential terrorists. The Patriot Act is the first major law to try to resolve this issue, but it will likely not be the last.

Chapter One

The Passage of the Patriot Act and Its Key Provisions

In the days after September 11, Bush and his attorney general, Ashcroft, quickly agreed on the need to introduce legislation to Congress that would enhance the FBI's ability to deal with the war on terror. Senior officials also saw this as an opportunity to pass legislation the department had been supporting for years—legislation that would loosen restrictions on how law enforcement agents operate. A body of federal law dating back to the 1950s had codified the procedures by which the FBI and other agencies were allowed to monitor phone calls, search suspects' homes, and eavesdrop on private conversations. These laws, as journalist Robert O'Harrow Jr. puts it, "defined and delimited the government's ability to snoop."[17]

The DOJ had been arguing for years that these laws were out of date and needed to be revised to deal with modern communication technologies, such as cell phones and the Internet, and modern threats, including terrorism. Congress had previously addressed some of these concerns with the Antiterrorism and Effective Death Penalty Act of 1996. Passed in response to the bombing of the World Trade Center in 1993 and the Oklahoma City bombing of 1995, the 1996 law eased federal restrictions on electronic surveillance and other search powers. It also made sixty new offenses, most of them terrorism-related, punishable by death. For the DOJ, the September 11 attacks showed that the United States needed to go even further in

On September 11, 2001, smoke billows from the north tower of the World Trade Center as a second plane strikes the south tower.

expanding law enforcement's power to combat terrorism.

Ashcroft too felt that the September 11 attacks were a turning point for the DOJ: "On September 11, the wheel of history turned and the world will never be the same," he said. "The fight against terrorism is now the first and overriding priority of the Department of Justice."[18] According to Assistant Attorney General Viet Dinh, Ashcroft felt that Congress should grant the DOJ "all that is necessary for law enforcement, within the bounds of the Constitution, to discharge the obligation to fight this war on terror."[19]

Mere days after the attacks—while the locations of Bush, Ashcroft, and other U.S. leaders were still being kept secret for security reasons—Dinh and his staff began putting together a first draft of what would eventually become the Patriot Act. On the evening of September 17, they faxed the legislation—initially known as the AntiTerrorism Act (ATA)—to select members of Congress. In this first draft, some of the law enforcement measures that the DOJ proposed were extremely powerful. They included very few restraints on federal investigators' authority to wiretap, search, and arrest individuals with little evidence. The most extreme provision allowed the government to detain suspected terrorists secretly and indefinitely, without a trial. As Steven Brill describes in *After: The Rebuilding and Defending of America in the September 12 Era,*

Most shocking was that the bill suspended what was known in the law as habeus corpus—which gave anyone detained on American soil the right to demand a court hearing to challenge the authority of those holding them. Lincoln had suspended habeus corpus for a time during the Civil War. Now Ashcroft proposed that it just plain be eliminated.[20]

Although many lawmakers were concerned about provisions such as these, everyone agreed that Congress needed to pass a counterterrorism bill. For the next six weeks, the bill that would become the Patriot Act was the subject of intense political negotiations.

Negotiating the Bill

On one side of the debate were Ashcroft, DOJ legal teams, and a large number of congresspeople who were ready to give them whatever powers they deemed necessary to fight terrorism. On the other side were civil liberties groups and legislators concerned about the bill's effects on individual freedom.

The dozens of civil liberties groups lobbying against the bill included the ACLU, the Electronic Privacy Information Center, and the American-Arab Anti-Discrimination Committee. ACLU Washington director Laura Murphy said their mission after September 11 was to prevent Congress from legislating "what they had tried to pass after Oklahoma City but had not gotten away with.... More wiretapping, more searches, less involvement of judges and warrants."[21] On September 18, these groups

19

"Entrust, but with Oversight"

On October 25, the day that Congress approved the final version of the Patriot Act, Senator Patrick Leahy gave a speech on the Senate floor in support of the legislation. He also stated his concerns about how the law would affect civil liberties and emphasized the need for Congress to monitor how the FBI and the Department of Justice use their new authority.

Let me talk for a few moments about the need for congressional oversight. This bill has raised serious and legitimate concerns about the expansion of authorities for government surveillance and intelligence gathering within this country. Indeed, this bill will change surveillance and intelligence procedures for all types of criminal and foreign intelligence investigations, not just for terrorism cases. Significantly, the sunset provision included in the final bill calls for vigilant legislative oversight, so that the Congress will know how these legal authorities are used and whether they are abused over the next four years. . . .

We have done our utmost to protect Americans against abuse of these new law enforcement tools. In granting these new powers, the American people and we, their representatives in Congress, also grant the Administration our trust that they will not be misused. Congressional oversight will be crucial in enforcing this compact. To paraphrase former President Reagan, we will entrust, but with oversight. The four-year sunset provision included in this final agreement will be an enforcement mechanism for adequate oversight.

---

issued a manifesto entitled "In Defense of Freedom at a Time of Crisis," which cautioned, "We should resist the temptation to enact proposals in the mistaken belief that anything that may be called anti-terrorist will necessarily provide greater security."[22] More than 150 organizations had signed the manifesto by October 2. However, as O'Harrow notes, "They also grasped the difficulty of their position. Here they were, trying to persuade Americans to hold fast to concerns about freedom and privacy, while the vast majority of people were terrified. Polls later showed that most people were more than willing to trade off civil liberties and privacy protections for more security."[23] Furthermore, these civil liberties groups' power was limited to their ability to influence members of Congress and the public—they were outsiders to the negotiations actually taking place on Capitol Hill.

The Patriot Act is unusual in that it is the product of direct negotiation between the White House and a few representatives of Congress. Normally, the executive branch submits a bill to Congress, and Congress makes changes to the legislation in a time-consuming committee-approval process. In the aftermath of September 11, parties on both sides agreed to direct negotiations instead. Ashcroft and Dinh represented the

DOJ and the Bush administration. Among the many legislators who had input on the negotiations, Senator Patrick Leahy (D-VT) and Representatives Dick Armey (R-TX) and Bob Barr (R-GA) stood out.

Leahy, the chief negotiator for the Senate, was considered the most liberal of the negotiators representing Congress and the most concerned with protecting civil liberties. "We do not want terrorists to win by having basic protections taken away from us," he said, and he pressed Ashcroft to compromise on a variety of issues. "We're trying to find a middle ground, and I think we can,"[24] he said of the negotiation process. It was in the House that the Patriot Act faced the most opposition, since the ACLU had forged an alliance with conservative and libertarian Republicans in the House, such as Barr and Armey. Under pressure from these representatives, Ashcroft was forced to remove some controversial measures—

Although Senator Patrick Leahy extended his support to the Patriot Act, he worried that the act's provisions could result in civil liberties violations.

such as the indefinite detention of suspected terrorists without trial—from the House version of the bill.

Frustrated by this compromise, on September 24 Ashcroft appeared before the House Judiciary Committee to urge passage of the Patriot Act. He warned that time was of the essence:

> The American people do not have the luxury of unlimited time in erecting the necessary defenses to future terrorist acts. . . . Every day that passes without dated statutes and the old rules of engagement . . . is a day that terrorists have a competitive advantage. Until Congress makes these changes, we are fighting an unnecessarily uphill battle.[25]

This call for action put pressure on Congress to wrap up negotiations and enact the bill into law.

The Patriot Act Becomes Law

The Senate passed the Patriot Act on the night of October 11 by a vote of 98-1, with Feingold dissenting and Senator Mary Landrieu (D-LA) not voting. The following morning, the House passed the bill by a vote of 337-66, with nine representatives not voting. Congress had approved the 342-page Patriot Act just thirty-one days after the September 11 attacks. This was extraordinarily fast for a law of the Patriot Act's scope. Several members of Congress complained that they did not have time to fully review the legislation. "Members had to vote on a multi-hundred page bill with no one having had a chance to read the bill except for staffs," said Representative John Conyers (D-MI). "The bill was available an hour in advance. People had to vote based on summaries."[26]

News of the Patriot Act's passage was overshadowed by the fall 2001 anthrax scare. Throughout October 2001, anonymous individuals mailed potentially lethal anthrax spores to several media outlets and to members of Congress. On October 15, Senate Majority Leader Tom Daschle received such a letter, and testing revealed twenty-eight members of his staff had been exposed to the bacteria. Amid confirmation of fifteen cases of inhalation anthrax among postal workers and media employees, the U.S. Capitol, Supreme Court, and State Department offices were closed for decontamination.

In this tense atmosphere, there were still some differences between the Senate and House versions of the Patriot Act that needed to be reconciled before the president could sign it into law. Most notably, Armey had succeeded in getting the House to include "sunset" provisions on some of the most controversial search and surveillance powers—after a period of four years, these provisions expire unless Congress renews them. In addition, the law contains two provisions designed to address civil libertarians' concerns. Section 1001 of the Patriot Act directs the inspector general of the DOJ to designate an official to review complaints about civil liberties abuses, and Section

Less than one month after September 11, post office employees are led to a decontamination area after letters containing anthrax spores passed through their facility.

1002 of the law states that "in the quest to identify, locate, and bring to justice the perpetrators and sponsors of the terrorist attacks . . . the civil rights and civil liberties of all Americans, including Sikh-Americans, should be protected."[27]

Congress approved the final version of the Patriot Act on October 25, and the president signed it into law the next day,

announcing in a formal Rose Garden ceremony, "Today, we take an essential step in defeating terrorism, while protecting the constitutional rights of all Americans. With my signature, this law will give intelligence and law enforcement officials important new tools to fight a present danger."[28] The day before, Ashcroft had given a speech praising the new law, in which he stated,

"The new tools for law enforcement in the war against terrorism are the products of hundreds of hours of consultation and careful consideration by the administration, members of Congress, and state and local officials. They are careful, balanced, and long overdue improvements in our capacity to prevent terrorism."[29] Addressing concerns about whether the Patriot Act curtailed civil liberties, Ashcroft declared:

The law enforcement campaign that will commence in earnest when the legislation is signed into law will be many years in duration. Some will ask whether a civilized nation—a nation of law and not of men—can use the law to defend itself from barbarians and remain civilized. Our answer, unequivocally, is "yes." Yes, we will defend civilization. And yes, we will

During the anthrax scare of October 2001, former attorney general John Ashcroft displays an FBI advisory that informs citizens on how to handle suspicious mail.

preserve the rule of law because it makes us civilized.[30]

New Crimes and Harsher Penalties

Throughout the debate, the Patriot Act's search and surveillance provisions were the main subject of negotiation and controversy. However, the sweeping law contains 153 separate provisions, many of which are much less controversial. For example, several of the Patriot Act's provisions define a broad array of terrorist activities as federal crimes. Attacking mass transportation facilities, possessing biological weapons, harboring terrorists, and money laundering to support terrorism are federal crimes under the Patriot Act. As Kettl writes in *System Under Stress: Homeland Security and American Politics*, "Federal officials were concerned that the ingenuity of terrorists had grown faster than criminal law, and they were intent on capturing the full range of terrorist activities as crimes."[31]

These provisions of the Patriot Act are intended to supplement existing law. In some cases, the Patriot Act clarifies or extends older laws. For example, previous laws made it a crime to harbor illegal aliens, those engaged in espionage, and felons. The Patriot Act explicitly establishes the harboring of terrorists as a punishable offense. In another example, previous federal statutes had made it a crime to use biological agents or toxins as weapons. The Patriot Act amends the definition of "for use as

a weapon," making it a crime to possess biological agents or toxins unless such possession can be justified for peaceful purposes. The Patriot Act also makes it a crime for convicted felons, illegal immigrants, and fugitives to possess biological toxins or agents. Such clarifications in the law should make it easier for the government to prosecute terrorists.

In other cases, the Patriot Act increases the penalties for previously defined crimes, particularly those involving the taking of human life. For example, the Patriot Act increases the maximum penalty for carrying a weapon or explosive onto an aircraft from fifteen to twenty years, or to life imprisonment if death results from the crime. It increases the penalty for sabotage of a nuclear facility from ten to twenty years, or to life if death results. Also, under federal law, there is a penalty of five years imprisonment for *conspiring* to commit any federal felony, in addition to the penalty for actually committing the crime. The Patriot Act increases the penalties for conspiring to commit a list of designated terrorist acts—such as causing a train wreck or killing while armed with a firearm inside a federal building—so that the penalties for conspiring to commit these crimes are as harsh as the penalties for actually committing them.

The Patriot Act extends the statute of limitations for terrorist crimes. For most federal crimes other than murder, prosecution must begin within five years after the crime occurs. Previous laws had raised the statute of limitations to eight years for

25

A soldier stands guard outside a maximum security facility at the Guantánamo Bay U.S. naval base, where suspected terrorists can be detained indefinitely.

crimes of terrorism. The Patriot Act eliminates the statute of limitations for any crime of terrorism that risks death or serious bodily injury, so that terrorists, like murderers, can be brought to justice even decades after committing their crimes.

Money Laundering and Computer Crime

One type of crime that the Patriot Act gives particular attention to is money laundering. Money laundering is the flow of "dirty"

money that is derived from, or used to commit, a crime. Money laundering is a major concern because, in the aftermath of September 11, federal investigators discovered that hundreds of thousands of dollars had flowed through U.S. financial networks to terrorist cells. For example, in some cases, funds that were donated to Muslim charity groups in the United States and Saudi Arabia were being funneled to terrorists. Less than two weeks after the September 11 attacks, Bush announced that international law enforcement agents had frozen more than $6 million in fifty bank accounts with ties to terrorist networks—thirty of them in the United States. In drafting the Patriot Act, the DOJ wanted stronger authority to trace the flow of money. "Without money, terrorist networks do not exist," explains Renaud Van Ruymbeke, a French financial crime prosecutor who worked with U.S. authorities after September 11. "They can't finance their operations overseas or purchase arms."[32]

The Patriot Act greatly expands previously existing regulations that require businesses to keep records of all financial transactions and to report suspicious activity to the government. It defines a number of new money-laundering crimes and increases penalties for existing crimes. The law empowers the government to confiscate money or other property derived from, or used to facilitate, terrorist activity. Several sections of the Patriot Act also instruct U.S. officials, such as the secretary of the treasury and the secretary of state, to work with foreign governments to develop systems to thwart money laundering.

Another crime that the Patriot Act specifically targets is computer crime. As Kettl explains,

Government officials increasingly worried that terrorists, or even ordinary hackers, would exploit vulnerabilities in the Internet to flood the system with e-mail or to damage computer records. With the growing dependence of the world economy on electronic commerce and communication, officials wanted to increase the system's protection against cyber-terror attacks.[33]

Previous laws had made computer fraud and abuse a crime; the Patriot Act increases the penalties for these crimes and instructs the attorney general and the Secret Service to establish a national network of electronic crime task forces.

Border Protection and Victims' Funds

One of the vulnerabilities that Congress and the Bush administration most wanted to address in drafting the Patriot Act was the ease with which foreign terrorists were able to enter the United States undetected. The Patriot Act tripled the number of border patrol, customs agents, and other personnel monitoring the U.S.-Canadian border. It also authorized $50 million in funds to upgrade border surveillance equipment, as well as funds to create a criminal record identification information system relating to visa applications to the United States. The Patriot Act also provides funding for an Internet-based system that confirms whether immigrants who come to the United States on student visas attend the colleges and universities they say they will.

The Patriot Act expands border agents' authority to refuse admission to the United States to individuals with ties to terrorism. It also empowers federal agents to deport immigrants who engage in terrorist activity, provide material support for a terrorist organization, or publicly endorse

The Broad Scope of the Patriot Act's Money-Laundering Provisions

Surprisingly, the provisions of the Patriot Act aimed at catching money launderers have proven to be almost as controversial as those that expand the FBI's wiretap authority. The law requires businesses to report suspicious customer activity to the government and gives federal investigators increased authority to search individual financial records.

Under Section 314 of the Patriot Act, law enforcement agencies can submit the name of any terror suspect to the Treasury Department, which then orders financial institutions across the country to search their records for any matches. "In effect," writes Michael Isikoff in a December 1, 2003, *Newsweek* article, "the Patriot Act allows the Feds to search every financial institution in the country for the records of anybody they have suspicions about—the very definition, critics say, of a fishing expedition."

In December 2003, *Newsweek* investigated the use of Section 213 and found that the government had conducted searches on 962 suspects. However, fully two-thirds of these searches were for money-laundering cases that had no apparent connection to terrorism. The Internal Revenue Service (IRS), for example, had initiated searches for tax evasion, and the postal service had used the law to investigate postal fraud. DOJ officials have defended these uses of the law, pointing out that money laundering is a federal crime. However, in a January 5, 2004, *Insight on the News* article by John Berlau, "Money Laundering and Mission Creep," former DOJ official Paul Rosenzweig sides with critics: "If we're using the new terrorism money-laundering laws to broaden our tax-cheat powers, that would be a mistake."

terrorist activities. These provisions are somewhat controversial because what constitutes "terrorist activity" or "terrorist organization" is very broadly defined in the Patriot Act. Among the provisions regarding immigrants, however, the most controversial is one that empowers the attorney general to detain, for up to seven days, any immigrant he has reasonable grounds to believe is a threat to national security.

Partly out of concern that these provisions of the Patriot Act might be perceived as antiforeigner, the law provides relief for foreigners who were victimized by the September 11 attacks. These provisions extend certain benefits and relax immigration restrictions for immigrants who lost family members or were otherwise affected by the September 11 attacks.

Most of the compensation for September 11 victims who are not immigrants came via the September 11 Victim Compensation Fund, which was passed before the Patriot Act. However, the Patriot Act also provided some extra relief for victims. It increased the benefit for police officers, firefighters, and ambulance and rescue personnel who are killed or disabled in the line of duty from $100,000 to $250,000. The Patriot Act also amends the Victim of Crime Act of 1984, providing guidelines for how victims of terrorism can be compensated under the federal Crime Victims Fund.

Other Procedural Changes and Funding Allocations

The Patriot Act contains a number of smaller procedural changes designed to support the war on terrorism. For example, the act removes previously existing limits on the amount of money that the government can offer as a reward for the capture of terrorists or for information in terrorism cases. It also allows the government to collect DNA samples from convicted terrorists for identification and forensic purposes.

Many provisions in the act provide funding for the war on terrorism. For example, the law provides $25 million a year through 2007 to state and local agencies to train police, firefighters, and medical rescue workers in responding to terrorist attacks; $50 million a year for the attorney general to develop regional computer forensic laboratories; and $150 million for building federal-state-local law enforcement information sharing systems. The act also

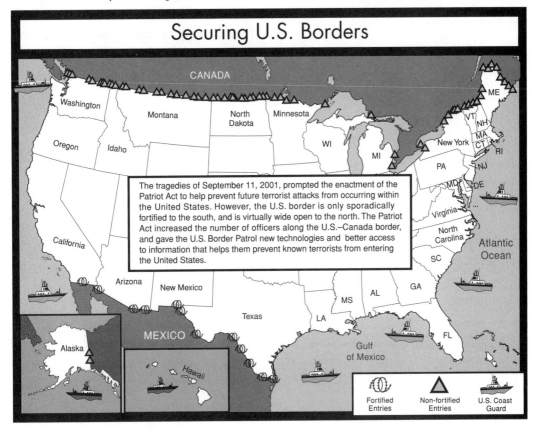

Securing U.S. Borders

The tragedies of September 11, 2001, prompted the enactment of the Patriot Act to help prevent future terrorist attacks from occurring within the United States. However, the U.S. border is only sporadically fortified to the south, and is virtually wide open to the north. The Patriot Act increased the number of officers along the U.S.–Canada border, and gave the U.S. Border Patrol new technologies and better access to information that helps them prevent known terrorists from entering the United States.

Fortified Entries — Non-fortified Entries — U.S. Coast Guard

increases funding for the FBI and establishes grants to aid state and local governments in enhancing their capacity to respond to terrorist attacks.

The Patriot Act contains numerous other miscellaneous provisions. "Many have little impact on the daily lives of most Americans," write Ann McFeatters and Karen MacPherson of the *Pittsburgh Post-Gazette.* "For example, the law allows money to be spent to re-establish a government office destroyed by terrorists. It condemns discrimination against Arab or Muslim Americans. It permits the FBI to hire more translators."[34]

An Omnibus Piece of Legislation

The Patriot Act is an omnibus piece of legislation—that is, it is a very broad law that deals with several different subjects and alters U.S. laws and policies in many different ways. The controversies that have surrounded the law since its passage are similarly wide-ranging. When journalists write editorials or politicians give speeches discussing the benefits of or the problems with the Patriot Act, it is important to ascertain which provisions of the law they are referring to. Even the Patriot Act's harshest critics acknowledge that many of its provisions are necessary, while its staunchest defenders also admit that no law as complex as the Patriot Act can be perfect. The provisions that the two groups disagree on most are those dealing with the government's search and surveillance powers, which defenders argue are crucial for the war on terrorism and critics warn are threats to Americans' constitutional freedoms.

Chapter Two

Expanded Surveillance Powers and the Fourth Amendment

The primary purpose of the Patriot Act is to loosen restrictions on law enforcement agents, making it easier for them to obtain warrants to tap terrorism suspects' phones, monitor their e-mail and Internet usage, search their homes and offices, and search their financial, educational, library, and other records. Bush, Ashcroft, and other DOJ officials have repeatedly stated that these expanded powers are crucial to the war on terrorism. Civil liberties groups, on the other hand, worry that the Patriot Act violates, or at least weakens, the Fourth Amendment.

The Fourth Amendment protects American citizens against unreason-

able searches and seizures. In practice, it means that law enforcement agents must obtain a warrant from a judge—by showing "probable cause" that a crime has been committed—in order to search a criminal suspect's home or place a wiretap on his phone. The principle behind the Fourth Amendment and the warrant system is that judicial oversight prevents law enforcement agents from abusing their search and surveillance powers. As law professor Stephen J. Schulhofer explains,

This constitutional regime is a concrete expression of our commitment to effective checks and balances. The Framers of the U.S. Constitution knew that without some outside control well-intentioned investigators would too quickly find "probable cause" and too easily abuse their power to search. The Fourth Amendment therefore requires that the judgment about probable cause ordinarily be made by a neutral judicial officer, who will narrowly define the permissible scope of the search before it occurs.[35]

Thus, the warrant system serves to balance the individual's right to freedom from government searches and surveillance against the government's need to investigate crimes.

Although the FBI suspected Zacarias Moussaoui of terrorist activities before September 11, the agency was unable to obtain warrants to monitor his activities.

The warrant system serves as a *restriction* on law enforcement agents: "Pre–Patriot Act law," writes political science professor Christopher Banks, "gave preference to safeguarding private telephone, face-to-face conversations, and electronic or computer messages . . . by prohibiting eavesdropping unless a warrant could be obtained in a set of narrowly defined circumstances."[36] In the aftermath of September 11, FBI and other government officials argued that current laws were too restrictive. They pointed to examples such as Zacarias Moussaoui, an alleged al Qaeda agent known to have aided the September 11 hijackers while they were in the United States. Prior to September 11, some FBI agents were suspicious of Moussaoui because he had attended a flight school where he inquired about whether cockpit doors could be opened during flight, and because he had spent time in Pakistan, where al Qaeda had recruited many operatives. But because the FBI could not demonstrate probable cause, it could not obtain a warrant to search Moussaoui's computer or tap his phone. "Consequently," writes Mark Reibling, author of a book on FBI-CIA relations, "the FBI lost its best chance to learn of Moussaoui's links to the other September 11 conspirators before they could strike."[37] The Patriot Act makes changes to the warrant system primarily by amending another law, the Foreign Intelligence Surveillance Act (FISA).

The FISA Court

Controversy over how to balance national security and Fourth Amendment concerns existed well before September 11. Throughout the twentieth century, there were many cases in which government agents used wiretaps and other surveillance tools without a warrant, when they felt that national security was at stake. In some cases, the FBI and the Central Intelligence Agency (CIA) spied on domestic political groups, in clear violation of the Fourth Amendment. In 1972, the Supreme Court ruled that the president's authority to see to national security did not justify using domestic wiretaps without a warrant: "The freedoms of the Fourth Amendment," stated the Court, "cannot properly be guaranteed if domestic security surveillances are conducted solely within the discretion of the Executive Branch, without the detached judgment of a neutral magistrate."[38] Six years later, Congress responded by passing FISA, an attempt to eliminate warrantless searches and regulate the relatively rare cases in which national security is at stake and law enforcement agents are either unable to procure a traditional warrant because they cannot show probable cause, or are unwilling to do so because the information is classified.

FISA established the Foreign Intelligence Surveillance Court. FBI agents can apply to the FISA court for a special FISA warrant to conduct searches or surveillance. The FISA court allows law enforcement agents to partially ignore the Fourth Amendment restriction of having to show probable cause that the search will reveal evidence of a crime. In addition, the FISA court operates in secret, and FISA warrants are therefore not subject to public scrutiny.

The Case for Wiretaps

Stuart Taylor Jr. is a writer for the National Journal. *In the following excerpt from his article "Rights, Liberties, and Security" in the Winter 2003* Brookings Review, *he makes the unusual argument that government wiretaps are not a major threat to civil liberties:*

Proposals to increase the government's wiretapping powers awaken fears of unleashing Orwellian thought police to spy on, harass, blackmail, and smear political dissenters and others. Libertarians point out that most conversations overheard and e-mails intercepted in the war on terrorism will be innocent and that the tappers and buggers will overhear intimacies and embarrassing disclosures that are none of the government's business.

Such concerns argue for taking care to broaden wiretapping and surveillance powers only as much as seems reasonable to prevent terrorist acts. But broader wire-tapping authority is not all bad for civil liberties. It is a more accurate and benign method of penetrating terrorist cells than the main alternative, which is planting and recruiting informers—a dangerous, ugly, and unreliable business in which the government is already free to engage without limit. The narrower the government's surveillance powers, the more it will rely on informants. . . .

It's also worth noting that despite the government's already-vast power to comb through computerized records of our banking and commercial transactions and much else that we do in the computer age, the vast majority of the people who have seen their privacy or reputations shredded have not been wronged by rogue officials. They have been wronged by media organizations, which do far greater damage to far more people with far less accountability.

The secret FISA court is sometimes referred to as a "spy" court, and FISA warrants essentially allow federal agents to sidestep the traditional warrant system. It is easy to forget that FISA was originally passed to try to regulate the warrantless searches and wiretaps that were already occurring. To this end, FISA included several restrictions intended to ensure that FISA warrants are used only in cases where national security is at stake. Most notably, under FISA's original terms, the FISA court would grant warrants only if the primary purpose of a search was to gather intelligence on "foreign powers and their agents," and these warrants were not to be used on American citizens unless he or she were "linked to foreign espionage."

Expanding FISA

The Patriot Act loosens these restrictions. Section 218 of the Patriot Act authorizes FBI agents to obtain FISA warrants in investigations where intelligence gathering is a "significant purpose" of the investigation rather than the primary purpose, and removes the requirement that the target of the search be "linked to foreign espionage." These small changes in wording greatly expand the types of cases that fall under the FISA court's jurisdiction. Government agents can now obtain FISA warrants in drug trafficking and other types of criminal investigations, as long as there is a significant chance they will learn something about a terror investigation.

Ashcroft argues that Section 218 "makes the utilization of wiretaps against terrorists much more workable,"[39] and the looser requirements will likely help investigators. But as Dahlia Lithwick and Julia Turner of *Slate* magazine explain, expanding FISA in this way undermines the original intent of the law: "FISA was a constitutional 'bargain' struck by a Congress concerned that the executive branch needs some special leeway for foreign intelligence surveillance without undermining American criminal procedures laid out in the Constitution. Broadening FISA so that it may be used against Americans . . . subverts that bargain."[40]

Several sections of the Patriot Act specify the types of wiretaps and searches that may now be authorized by the FISA court. For example, Section 214 of the law says that the FISA court may approve the use of "pen register" and "trap and trace" wiretaps. (Pen registers monitor the numbers dialed from a suspect's telephone, while trap and trace devices monitor the source of incoming calls. They are limited forms of wiretap, and do not reveal the content of a suspect's conversation.) FISA had previously limited the use of these devices to facilities used by foreign agents or terrorists; under Section 218, these types of wiretaps may be used as long as the information resulting from them may help a terror investigation.

Internet Surveillance

Some of the most interesting and controversial provisions in the Patriot Act are those that deal with the Internet, cell phones, and other modern communications technologies. Prior to the Patriot Act, federal wiretap law had been rooted in Title III of the 1968 Omnibus Crime Control and Safe Streets Act. Title III details how and in what circumstances warrants may be issued for monitoring phone lines and private, face-to-face conversations, but it was written well before the Internet was an aspect of everyday life. Before the Patriot Act, government surveillance of the Internet was largely unregulated. Law enforcement agents applying for a warrant to monitor a suspect's Internet usage could only hope that the judge in question would agree that Title III applied to the Internet as well as phone lines. Furthermore, different judges might have different interpretations of how Title III applied to computers and the Internet, greatly complicating investigations.

In drafting the Patriot Act, one of the DOJ's main goals was to update federal wiretap law for the Internet era. One year after the law passed, Deputy Assistant Attorney General Alice Fisher argued that this aspect of the Patriot Act was vital to the war on terror:

> The USA PATRIOT Act allowed us to modernize our badly outmoded surveillance tools. Terrorists engaged in covert multinational operations use advanced technology, particularly in their communications and planning. While terrorists who were plotting against our nation traveled across the globe, carrying laptop computers and using disposable cell phones, federal investigators operated under laws seemingly frozen in an era of telegrams and switchboard operators. . . . The USA PATRIOT Act modernized existing law, and gave investigators crucial new tools.[41]

From a civil liberties perspective, the effects of the Patriot Act's "modernization" are mixed. For example, Section 216 of the law clarifies that pen register and trap and trace devices may be used to monitor Internet communications. On the one hand, it is good to finally have a federal law regulating the use of Internet wiretaps, since judges have been authorizing them for years. On the other hand, the Patriot Act is the first federal law explicitly to authorize Internet surveillance, something that computer privacy groups have been fighting since the Internet was first created.

A specific issue with Section 216 is that it is unclear exactly how these devices may be used for Internet surveillance. When used on phone lines, investigators with a pen register or trap and trace warrant may only monitor the numbers dialed into and out of a specific phone; they are not permitted to listen in on conversations. Similarly, Section 216 states that when these devices are used to monitor Internet communications, they may not be used to intercept the "content" of such communications. However, the Patriot Act does not specify what "content" means. For example, it may mean that investigators can monitor the sender and recipient of an e-mail, but not read the e-mail's content. But does it mean that if investigators are monitoring a suspect's Web surfing, they can keep track of the sites the suspect visits, but not read the contents of those sites? Internet privacy groups such as the Electronic Frontier Foundation (EFF) have repeatedly contacted the DOJ, requesting answers to such questions. In January 2005, the EFF sent a letter complaining that "the DOJ has refused to answer the public's very simple question: 'Can the government see what I'm reading on the web without having to show probable cause?' Yet the public's interest in an answer to that question, which implicates the most profound constitutional rights, is inestimable."[42]

Roving and Nationwide Wiretaps

Another way in which the Patriot Act seeks to modernize wiretap and warrant law is by expanding the scope of FISA warrants. Prior to the Patriot Act, most wiretap warrants could be issued only for a specific phone or computer, and a separate warrant had to be procured for each device that a suspect used. Over the years this has become a bigger and bigger problem for investigators, as people increasingly use multiple cell phones and computers in the course of their daily lives.

Laws passed in the 1980s and 1990s allow the FBI to obtain special warrants to install a wiretap on any communications device that a suspect uses. However, these "roving" wiretaps were authorized only in special circumstances, such as when the sus-

pect was involved in organized crime or when investigators could demonstrate that the suspect was intentionally changing phones to evade a wiretap. Section 206 of the Patriot Act allows the FISA court to issue warrants for roving wiretaps with far fewer restrictions and, as with other FISA warrants, investigators do not have to demonstrate probable cause that the suspect has committed a crime.

Fisher justified this provision: "This new authority allows us to avoid unnecessary cat-and-mouse games with terrorists

The Patriot Act eases restrictions on roving wiretaps of phones and computers belonging to suspected terrorists.

The Patriot Act's Civil Liberties Safeguards

In response to criticisms that the Patriot Act weakens the warrant system and other civil liberties protections, on March 7, 2005, Attorney General Alberto Gonzales gave a speech in which he emphasized several of the safeguards contained in the law:

What is often left out of the critics' accusations are the many safeguards built into the law itself.

The Patriot Act, for example, requires judicial approval for delayed notification search warrants. Courts can only allow these search warrants in the face of threats such as the death or physical harm to an individual, evidence tampering, witness intimidation. At all times, the government is subject to the jurisdiction and supervision of a federal judge.

The Patriot Act requires investigators to apply and receive federal court permission to obtain routing information such as incoming, outgoing phone numbers from the phone. There is no collection of the content of the communication....

The Patriot Act allows individuals recourse if they believe their rights were abused. In addition, the Justice Department's inspector general is required by law to review information and complaints alleging abuses under the Patriot Act.

Finally, the act requires me every six months to report to Congress the number of applications made for orders requiring the production of business records under the Patriot Act.

As these examples illustrate, this law not only fully respects the rights and liberties of America, but contains built-in safeguards that ensure the protection of our rights.

---

who are trained to thwart surveillance by rapidly changing hotels or residences, cell phones, and Internet accounts before important meetings or communications."[43] However, civil liberties groups warn that roving wiretaps could result in the government tapping dozens of public phones and computers, potentially violating the privacy and Fourth Amendment rights of other people who use them.

Closely related to Section 206 are Sections 219 and 220, which authorize judges to issue wiretaps for use outside their jurisdiction. Pre–Patriot Act laws required investigators to obtain separate warrants from different federal judges if a suspect moved from one region of the country to another. This was particularly a problem for Internet surveillance: If a suspect used a computer in one part of the country, but his Internet service provider's servers were located in another region, investigators had to obtain separate warrants from judges in both regions to, for example, search the suspect's e-mail. Sections 219 and 220 of the Patriot Act allow federal judges to issue warrants "without geographic limitation."[44]

Civil libertarians' primary objection to Sections 206, 219, and 220 is, again, that these changes weaken the warrant system and the Fourth Amendment. The purpose of the warrant system is to enable a judge to oversee the search and surveillance process and ensure that law enforcement agents do not abuse their powers. When warrants are issued for multiple phones and

Attorney General Alberto Gonzalez believes the Patriot Act contains a number of safeguards to prevent civil liberties violations.

Fundamental Disagreements

At the heart of the debate over the Patriot Act is a fundamental disagreement between law enforcement and civil libertarians about how much authority the government should have. The following excerpts, from the Department of Justice's Preserving Life & Liberty Web site and the Center for Democracy and Technology's brochure "What's Wrong with the Patriot Act and How to Fix It," demonstrate this division:

Sneak-and-Peek Searches

Preserving Life & Liberty: Federal courts in narrow circumstances long have allowed law enforcement to delay for a limited time when the subject is told that a judicially-approved search warrant has been executed.... These delayed notification search warrants have been used for decades, have proven crucial in drug and organized crime cases, and have been upheld by courts as fully constitutional.

CDT: Secret searches should be allowed only in special circumstances, such as if someone's life is at stake or evidence will be destroyed. Otherwise, FBI agents should have to knock on a person's door and announce that they have a search warrant, as intended by the Fourth Amendment.

Roving Wiretaps

Life & Liberty: For years, law enforcement has been able to use "roving wiretaps" to investigate ordinary crimes, including drug offenses and racketeering. . . . The Act authorized agents to seek court permission to use the same techniques in national security investigations to track terrorists.

CDT: The FBI should be granted wiretap orders only where it specifies either the name of the target or telephone or computer to be tapped.

---

computers and used nationwide, abuses are more likely to go unnoticed.

Secret Searches

One of the more controversial provisions of the Patriot Act is Section 213, which allows federal investigators to conduct so-called sneak-and-peek searches. Normally, police must attempt to notify a suspect of their intention to search before executing a warrant. According to Stanley and Steinhardt of the ACLU, "Such notice is a crucial check on the government's power because

it forces the authorities to operate in the open and allows the subject of searches to challenge their validity in court."[45] In sneak-and-peek searches, covert searches of a suspect's home or office are conducted without notifying the target until well after the search has been completed. The DOJ argues that secret searches are necessary because "in some cases if criminals are tipped off too early to an investigation, they might flee, destroy evidence, intimidate or kill witnesses, cut off contact with associates, or take other action to evade arrest."[46] Federal law had allowed secret searches in certain narrowly defined circumstances, and FISA had previously authorized sneak-and-peek warrants for intelligence investigations. Section 213 of the Patriot Act authorizes the FISA court to issue sneak-and-peek warrants in criminal investigations, even those that have nothing to do with terrorism.

Another of the Patriot Act's most controversial provisions is Section 215, under which the attorney general can gain access to an individual's library, financial, travel, video rental, phone, medical, church, synagogue, mosque, and other records without the target's knowledge or consent. The attorney general need only certify to the FISA court that the search protects against terrorism. The DOJ maintains that this power is merely an extension of existing laws that allow grand juries to subpoena a suspect's business records. The main differences are first, that Section 215 applies to any type of private record, and second, that under Section 215 such searches are secret. As the ACLU notes, "A gag order in the law prevents anyone served with a Section 215 order from telling anyone else that the FBI demanded information. Because the gag order remains in effect forever, surveillance targets—even wholly innocent ones—are *never* notified that their privacy has been compromised."[47]

Finally, one provision of the Patriot Act circumvents the warrant system entirely. Section 505 of the law authorizes the attorney general to issue "national security letters" to banks, telephone companies, and Internet service providers, requiring them to turn over an individual's financial, phone, or e-mail records. Previously, national security letters could be used only against individuals suspected of espionage, but Section 505 authorizes their use in any type of investigation. Like Section 215, those providing the records are gagged from revealing that a search took place, but unlike Section 215, Section 505 does not require even a FISA warrant.

While the DOJ stated in September 2003 that it had not made use of Section 215 since the Patriot Act had been passed, the attorney general has issued hundreds of national security letters under Section 505. The government has kept classified the details of whom the letters were issued to and why. What is known is that in September 2004, a federal judge struck down Section 505 of the Patriot Act as unconstitutional. An Internet service company (whose identity has been kept secret) had contested a national security letter forcing it to reveal customers' records. U.S. District Judge Victor Marrero agreed, ruling that Section 505 infringes on individuals' right to be free from unreasonable searches under the Fourth Amendment, and that the law's gag provision violates free speech rights under the First Amendment. The government is expected to appeal the decision.

More Questions than Answers

The types of searches and wiretaps authorized in the Patriot Act will certainly help investigators, but they may also weaken Americans' Fourth Amendment rights.

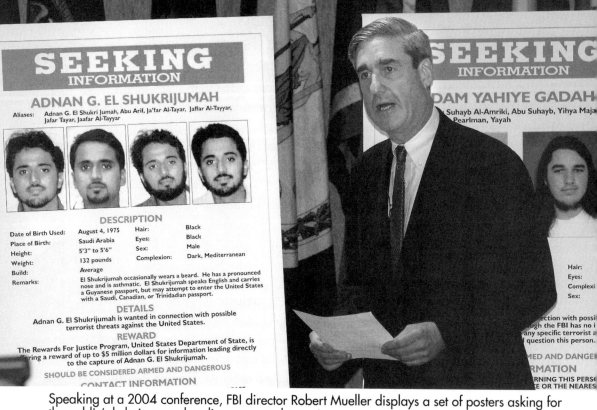

Speaking at a 2004 conference, FBI director Robert Mueller displays a set of posters asking for the public's help in apprehending suspected terrorists.

These provisions of the Patriot Act raise difficult questions not only about how to balance individual privacy with the need to investigate terrorism, but also about how wiretap law should be adapted to deal with modern communications technologies, and how much government secrecy is justified in the war on terror.

The questions that the Patriot Act raises about the Fourth Amendment are so difficult because there clearly *is* a need for the government to be able to invade individu-als' privacy in order to apprehend terrorists and ensure public safety. As sociologist Amitai Etzioni writes, the Fourth Amendment "is not phrased in terms as absolute as the First Amendment. It does not state that Congress 'shall make no law allowing search and seizure' or anything remotely like it. It states that there be no *un*reasonable searches."[48] In the war on terror, it is up to the American people, their elected officials, and the courts to determine which antiterrorism measures are reasonable and which are not.

Chapter Three

First Amendment and Immigrant Rights

The main purpose of the Patriot Act is to expand federal agents' authority to investigate and prosecute terrorists. The law makes it easier for investigators to tap phone lines, monitor individuals' Internet usage, and search suspects' homes and offices. Thus, from a civil liberties perspective, the Patriot Act infringes most on individual privacy and the Fourth Amendment's protection against unreasonable searches.

However, two other aspects of the law have garnered just as much controversy as these privacy and Fourth Amendment concerns. First, civil libertarians argue that the Patriot Act undermines the First Amendment's guarantees of free speech, a free press, and free association. Second, critics of the law maintain that it deprives immigrants of their due process and First Amendment rights.

A History of Suppressing Dissent

Civil liberties groups have focused so much on the Patriot Act's effects on First Amendment and immigrant rights because, historically, these have been the two civil liberties that the U.S. government has curtailed most in times of war and crisis.

As early as 1798, when U.S. leaders feared that war with France was imminent, Congress passed the Sedition Act, which made it a crime to criticize the government, and the Alien Act, which authorized the imprisonment and deportation of immigrants. The war with France never came, but the precedent of suppressing dissent and targeting immigrants in times of crisis was set. In 1917 and 1918, the United States passed another Sedition Act, this time to suppress dissent against America's involvement in

In June 1954, Senator Joseph McCarthy points to a large map indicating the locations of alleged Communists. Under McCarthy, hundreds of suspected Communists were targeted.

World War I. More than one thousand people were imprisoned for protesting the war, and hundreds of immigrants were deported.

After World War I, the Supreme Court made it clear that laws such as the Sedition Acts are unconstitutional. However, more recent, less blatant curtailments of the First Amendment have also occurred. At the height of the Cold War in the late 1940s and early 1950s, the House Un-American Activities Committee (HUAC) began investigating organizations that secretly supported communism and exposing individuals with ties to such organizations. Many of these individuals had committed no crime. In persecuting individuals because of their political beliefs and the people they associate with, HUAC undermined the First Amendment's guarantees of free speech and free association. The committee also ruined many individuals' lives and careers, since persons targeted by HUAC were blacklisted within their respective industries. This "Red Scare" reached its height in 1953, when Joseph McCarthy (R-WI), chairman of the Senate counterpart to HUAC, was rebuked on live television for berating a witness. A year later, the Senate censured McCarthy for dishonorable conduct, but HUAC continued similar investigations for several years.

Many civil libertarians feel that the worst result of the Red Scare was the general chilling of free speech that the persecution created. For every individual who was brought before Congress, countless others hesitated to voice any unpatriotic sentiment, for fear that they might come under suspicion themselves. Arthur Miller captured this oppressive atmosphere in his 1953 play *The Crucible*, in which the seventeenth-century Salem witch trials serve as an allegory of persecution. The term "McCarthyism" is still used to describe a "witch hunt" in which the targets are individuals with unpopular political beliefs.

Many civil liberties groups worry that in the war on terrorism, a new kind of McCarthyism might take hold. Nadine Strossen, president of the ACLU, sees

> parallels between what we're going through now and McCarthyism.... The term "terrorism" is taking on the same kind of characteristics as the

term "communism" did in the 1950s. It stops people in their tracks, and they're willing to give up their freedoms. People are too quickly panicked. They are too willing to give up their rights and to scapegoat people, especially immigrants and people who criticize the war.[49]

In particular, the ACLU and other groups argue that certain provisions of the Patriot Act may chill free speech and undermine the First Amendment.

Snooping Through Library Records?

One provision of the Patriot Act that concerns free speech advocates is Section 215, which empowers the government to search individuals' financial, library, medical, phone, and other records without the individuals' knowledge or approval. In particular, the prospect of government agents monitoring which books people purchase from bookstores or borrow from the library alarms groups such as the ACLU and the American Library Association (ALA). In January 2003 the ALA issued a resolution stating that the Patriot Act presents "danger to the constitutional rights and privacy rights of library users."[50] Patricia Schroeder, president of the Association of American Publishers, says that "Section 215 seriously undermines the First Amendment-protected activities of authors and publishers, booksellers and librarians, and indeed anyone who reads."[51]

When the First and Fourth Amendments Intersect

In the 1972 case of United States v. United States District Court for the Eastern District of Michigan, *the Supreme Court recognized that unrestricted government surveillance raises both free speech (First Amendment) and privacy (Fourth Amendment) issues. The case revolved around President Richard Nixon's contention that the executive branch should be permitted to use wiretaps, without a court-approved warrant, to investigate national security threats posed by domestic groups. The Court ruled that such cases reflect "a convergence of First and Fourth Amendment values not present in 'ordinary' crime," and rejected the Nixon administration's claim. In its ruling, the Court stated that the government would be* tempted to use claims about national security to silence political dissent:

Official surveillance, whether its purpose be criminal investigation or ongoing intelligence gathering, risks infringement of constitutionally protected privacy of speech. Security surveillances are especially sensitive because of the inherent vagueness of the domestic security concept, the necessarily broad and continuing nature of intelligence gathering, and the temptation to utilize such surveillances to oversee political dissent.

In loosening the restrictions on government surveillance and searches, the Patriot Act reopens these questions about how to balance national security with Americans' First and Fourth Amendment rights.

The controversy over Section 215 shows how privacy and First Amendment issues sometimes intersect. The First Amendment's guarantee of a free press has been interpreted as protecting individuals' access to public information in general. As the *San Francisco Chronicle* explains, "Our founders understood the value of open access to knowledge. One of the measures of a great democracy is the ability of ordinary citizens to explore ideas without government interference."[52] Section 215 of the Patriot Act does not restrict the types of books that individuals can read, but civil libertarians worry that, if the government is secretly monitoring what people read, people will

censor themselves. Thus, when it comes to what people read and write, lack of privacy has First Amendment implications. As librarian Robin Rice puts it, the problem with Section 215 is "the chilling effect on information-seekers when users are concerned that their privacy will not be protected."[53]

Section 215 raises First Amendment concerns in another way. According to the provision, if the FBI orders a librarian or bookseller to turn over records on an individual, the librarian or bookseller is forbidden to tell anyone about the search. Not only may the librarian or bookseller not inform the individual whose records have been searched, but he or she is also prohibited from telling the media about the FBI's activities. Therefore, according to the ACLU, "The provision violates the First Amendment by prohibiting those served with Section 215 orders from disclosing that fact to others, even where there is no real need for secrecy."[54]

The DOJ has firmly defended Section 215 against these criticisms. First, although Patriot Act supporters such as lawyer James Zirin have argued that terrorists could use books to aid in terrorist activities— "If someone starts reading cookbooks on how to build a dirty bomb, isn't that something the authorities should look into?"[55]—DOJ officials have denied that Section 215 might be used to search library records, and indeed the word "library" does not appear in the Patriot Act. "The law enforcement community has no interest in your reading habits,"[56] according to Ashcroft.

Second, the DOJ emphasizes a passage in Section 215 that states that searches of individuals' records cannot be initiated "solely upon the basis of activities protected by the First Amendment."[57] That is, federal officials must have some reason to suspect an individual of having terrorist ties *before* searching his or her records under Section 215.

Finally, defenders of Section 215 point out that oversight mea-

sures in the Patriot Act require the attorney general to report to Congress every six months on how Section 215 is being used. On October 17, 2002, in its first annual review of how the DOJ was implementing

President Richard Nixon believed the executive branch should be permitted to use wiretaps without court-approved warrants.

Section 215, the House Judiciary Committee found nothing to give rise to "to any concern that the authority is being misused or abused."[58]

Nevertheless, the DOJ has been reluctant to release specific details to the public about how Section 215 has been used. In October 2002, the ACLU and other groups used the Freedom of Information Act, a 1966 law designed to reduce government secrecy that serves as an important tool for government watchdog groups, to file a request for information about how the government was using Section 215. A federal judge denied the request. Finally, in response to mounting criticisms of Section 215 and the secrecy surrounding it, in September 2003 the DOJ announced that it had

Civil libertarians warn that the Patriot Act greatly expands the government's authority to search individuals' library records.

Ashcroft Defends Section 215

In a September 15, 2003, speech, Attorney General John Ashcroft dismissed concerns that the FBI might use Section 215 to search the library records of average Americans.

Some have convinced the American Library Association that under the bipartisan Patriot Act, the FBI is not fighting terrorism. Instead, agents are checking how far you have gotten on the latest Tom Clancy novel.

Now you may have thought with all this hysteria and hyperbole, something had to be wrong. Do we at the Justice Department really care what you are reading? No. The law enforcement community has no interest in your reading habits. Tracking reading habits would betray our high regard for the First Amendment. And even if someone in the government wanted to do so, it would represent an impossible workload and a waste of law enforcement resources. . . .

With only 11,000 FBI agents in the entire country, it is simply ridiculous to think we could or would track what citizens are reading. I am not in a position to know, but according to the American Library Association there are more than 117,400 libraries in the United States. The American Library Association tells me that Americans visit our nation's libraries more than one billion times a year—1,146,284,000, to be exact. While there, they check out nearly two billion books a year—l,713,967,000, to be precise.

The hysteria is ridiculous. Our job is not.

---

not used the search powers granted in Section 215 *at all* in the two years since the Patriot Act had been passed. However, this announcement only partially mollified critics, who maintain that the potential for abuse of Section 215 still exists.

Defining Terrorism

Another aspect of the Patriot Act that concerns civil libertarians is its broad definition of terrorism. In particular, Section 802 of the Patriot Act is titled "Definition of Domestic Terrorism" and reads in part: "'Domestic terrorism' means activities that . . . involve acts dangerous to human life that are a violation of the criminal laws of the United States or of any State" as well as activities that "appear to be intended . . . to influence the policy of a government by intimidation or coercion."[59]

Civil liberties groups are concerned that, under this definition, political protesters could be prosecuted as terrorists. As Nancy Chang of the Center for Constitutional Rights explains,

Vigorous protest activities, by their very nature, could be construed as acts that "appear to be intended . . . to influence the policy of a government by intimidation or coercion." Further, clashes between demonstrators and police officers and acts of

Former attorney general John Ashcroft has vehemently denied that the government has any interest in accessing the library records of ordinary citizens.

civil disobedience—even those that do not result in injuries and are entirely non-violent—could be construed as "dangerous to human life" and in "violation of the criminal laws."[60]

ACLU spokesperson Rachel King argues that "groups like Greenpeace clearly engage in activities where they're violating the law and could in fact be creating situations dangerous to human life,"[61] since in the course of their environmental protests they have sometimes trespassed, obstructed development projects, and sabotaged whaling ships. At the other end of the political spectrum, conservative groups such as the Eagle Forum have expressed concern that Operation Rescue protestors, who engage in sit-ins to bar pregnant women from abortion facilities, could also be prosecuted as terrorists.

Defenders of the Patriot Act maintain that these concerns are wildly overblown. The DOJ has firmly denied accusations that peaceful protestors could be prosecuted under the Patriot Act:

Peaceful political discourse and dissent is one of America's most cherished freedoms, and is not subject to investigation as domestic terrorism. Under the Patriot Act, the definition of "domestic terrorism" is limited to conduct that (1) violates federal or state criminal law and (2) is dangerous to human life. Therefore, peaceful political organizations engaging in political advocacy will obviously not come under this definition.[62]

Lithwick and Turner of *Slate* magazine write that "the fears of this provision are almost entirely hypothetical."[63] As of early 2005, no political protestor has been charged under Section 802.

Fewer Protections for Immigrants

In general, even many critics of the Patriot Act believe that public outcry against abuse of American citizens' right to free speech, free assembly, and a free press would be so strong that enforcement of the Patriot Act would be kept in check. As Senator Carl Levin (D-MI) notes, "History is a powerful teacher. . . . I think there's a greater awareness of McCarthyism and there's a greater resistance against those who would try to still voices that they disagree with."[64] Overt attempts by the gov-

ernment to weaken Americans' First Amendment rights are likely to be politically very unpopular.

However, government efforts to curtail the rights of noncitizens have historically met with less opposition. For example, on June 2, 1919, a series of labor strikes and riots culminated in the explosion of bombs in eight cities, one outside the home of

Civil liberties groups worry that political protesters, like these members of Greenpeace, could be prosecuted as domestic terrorists under the Patriot Act.

Attorney General A. Mitchell Palmer. Thousands of people, most of them noncitizen immigrants, were arrested in the weeks that followed. Many were arrested, and hundreds deported, solely because of their affiliation with Communist, Socialist, or anarchist groups. This violated the First Amendment's prohibition of government discrimination against individuals based on the viewpoints they hold or the religious or political groups with which they associate. But because the Palmer raids targeted primarily immigrants, they met with limited public outcry.

Civil liberties groups maintain that the Patriot Act also violates the due process and First Amendment rights of noncitizens. One provision in particular, Section 411 of the act, has received the most criticism. Mainly, this section expands the types of offenses for which immigrants may be deported. Section 411 empowers the government to deport immigrants who "engage in terrorist activity,"[65] but as with Section 802, civil liberties groups take issue with the Patriot Act's broad definition of terrorism.

Under Section 411, noncitizens may be deported for being members of, or soliciting funds for, a terrorist organization. It does not matter if the organization engages in lawful political or humanitarian ends, or if the organization has not been formally designated as a terrorist organization by the government. It also does not matter if the immigrant in question had no knowledge of the organization's unlawful activities. The ACLU warns that Section 411 "creates a very serious risk that truly innocent individuals could be deported for truly innocent association with political groups that the government later chooses to regard as terrorist organizations.... Guilt by association is generally forbidden under the First Amendment and the history of McCarthyism shows the very real dangers of abuse."[66]

In addition to expanding the government's power to deport immigrants, Section 411 also bars individuals from entering the United States if they have ties to or have endorsed a terrorist group. The Center for Constitutional Rights argues that this provision undermines the First Amendment because it could restrict Americans' exposure to individuals with controversial political views:

This restriction is similar to that used in the [1952] McCarran-Walter Act—the law which denied entry into the country to any foreign national associated with a communist party or movement. Many prominent scholars and intellectuals were banned from this country because of their perceived association with communism.... It is highly likely that similar cases will occur under Section 411, diluting debate and the free exchange of ideas within our borders, and limiting many opportunities to engage with the peoples of the world.[67]

Section 411 is part of the government's broader effort to gain more control over who enters the United States, an effort

A U.S. Border Patrol agent in Florida takes a photo of a woman entering the country. Under the Patriot Act, the government is working to maintain tighter control over immigrants.

prompted by the fact that all nineteen of the September 11 hijackers were immigrants. As former Colorado governor Richard Lamm argues, "It is now imperative that we better monitor who we admit into this country."[68] The view that immigration and border control are key arenas in the war on terrorism was further established in March 2003, when the federal Immigration and Naturalization Service (INS) was dissolved and immigration control duties were transferred to the newly created Department of Homeland Security (DHS).

Nevertheless, the Supreme Court, in its 1896 decision in *Wong v. United States*, ruled that immigrants as well as a citizens are protected by the Bill of Rights. More recently, the Court ruled in the 2001 case *Zafvydas v. Davis* that although illegal immigrants are subject to deportation, they are entitled in deportation proceedings to due process and equal treatment under the law. The treatment of immigrants under Section 411 of the Patriot Act is a prime example of the tension between national security and the goal of keeping terrorists out of the country on the one hand, and the free speech and free association rights of individual immigrants on the other.

Detention of Noncitizens

Another controversial provision in the Patriot Act is Section 412, which empowers the attorney general to order the detention of an immigrant for up to seven days before bringing criminal charges. The detention of immigrants without trial became a very controversial issue after September 11. In the days after the attacks, the federal government rounded up over seven hundred immigrants. Most were soon released, but more than one hundred of the detainees were held for an average of two months.

In 2003 protesters in Portland demonstrate for the release of Mike Hawash, an immigrant detained as a material witness under the Patriot Act.

During this time, they were subjected to harsh living conditions and their names were not released to the public. The Fifth Amendment states that "no person shall be . . . deprived of life, liberty, or property, without due process of law," and civil libertarians charged that the detention of immigrants after September 11 was a clear violation of this due process clause. However, in the debate over the treatment of immigrants after September 11, it is important to remember that the Patriot Act had not yet been passed and therefore did not authorize the post–September 11 roundups.

Nevertheless, civil libertarians argue that Section 412 is too broad and prone to abuse. The provision empowers the attorney general to order the detention of any immigrant who he has "reasonable grounds to believe"[69] endangers national security. No judge may deny the attorney general's order, and the attorney general is not required to share the evidence he has for giving the order. Furthermore, the attorney general is empowered to hold the individual indefinitely if, after seven days, there is no country willing to accept the immigrant. If an individual were to be held indefinitely without being charged with a crime, it would be a severe violation of the Fifth Amendment. Chang of the Center for Constitutional Rights writes that "it is hard to avoid the conclusion that [Section 412] will deprive non-citizens of their liberty without due process of law."[70]

The Patriot Act does require the DOJ to report to Congress biannually on how Section 412 is implemented. As of early 2005, no immigrant has been detained under Section 412. In addition, Sections 411 and 412 of the Patriot Act will expire in December 2005 unless Congress renews them.

Protecting Civil Liberties in Times of Crisis

A key part of the war on terrorism is the ability of the government to identify individuals who are threats to national security. But as in past conflicts, this ability must be balanced with the right to dissent and the rights of immigrants. The provisions in the Patriot Act that raise concerns about First Amendment and immigrant rights are the latest chapter in the historic debate over how to balance security and civil liberties during times of crisis.

Chapter Four

The Changing Role of the FBI

In expanding federal law enforcement agents' search and surveillance powers, the Patriot Act initiated a fundamental shift in the mission of the Federal Bureau of Investigation. Before September 11, the FBI's role was to protect public safety by solving crimes and bringing criminals to justice. In the war on terrorism, however, the FBI's role is to identify and apprehend terrorists *before* they strike, by gathering intelligence on suspicious individuals and groups. As Etzioni writes, "The most important change in law enforcement since September 11, 2001 is that the FBI ... has shifted focus and procedure away from prosecution to prevention, from collecting information after a crime has been committed to preventing terrorist attacks from taking place."[71]

This is a major shift. In the two decades before September 11, there was a clear distinction between federal law enforcement agencies, such as the FBI and the Drug Enforcement Administration (DEA), and intelligence-gathering or "spy" agencies, such as the Central Intelligence Agency (CIA) and the National Security Agency (NSA). Law enforcement agencies solved crimes and brought criminals to justice, while intelligence agencies worked to counter preemptively threats to national security. The FBI operated domestically and was bound by the rules of criminal justice procedures, while the CIA operated mostly abroad and had much more freedom. The two agencies were discouraged from sharing information with one another, and formal prohibitions on doing so existed. This division is often described as a wall that separated intelligence gathering from law enforcement. For example, Attorney General Alberto Gonzales (who succeeded Ashcroft in 2005) has described the division as an "artificial and unwise bureaucratic wall that discouraged the sharing of information between law enforcement and the intelligence community."[72]

Why the Wall Was Set Up

Civil libertarians contend that this wall was put in place for good reason. As *Time* reporters Michael Duffy and Nancy Gibbs write, the restrictions on information sharing between intelligence and law enforcement agencies were "designed in response to the ugly days when dossiers were built, surveillance kept and blackmail threats held over the heads of people whose only crime was to criticize the U.S. government."[73] The wall between law enforcement and intelligence gathering was created as a response to the government's abuse of search and

In 2003 agents from a joint terrorist task force remove evidence from the office of a foreign national suspected of having terrorist ties.

surveillance powers in the 1940s, 50s, 60s, and 70s. In 1940, Roosevelt authorized Attorney General Robert H. Jackson to approve wiretaps on "persons suspected of subversive activities against the Government of the United States."[74] For the next three decades, without any guidance from Congress or the courts, the FBI gathered intelligence on private citizens without any individualized suspicion that the targets were engaged in criminal activity. The CIA, created in 1947, also operated in the domestic sphere during this period. The distinction between law enforcement and intelligence operations was blurred, and the two agencies worked together to monitor individuals and groups who might pose a threat to national security.

In the 1940s and 1950s, the FBI and CIA monitored primarily suspected Com-

Throughout the 1960s, the FBI kept Martin Luther King Jr. and other civil rights activists under close surveillance.

munists and Socialists. In the 1960s, under an FBI program called Cointelpro, the list of people spied on grew to include civil rights organizations and Vietnam War protestors who, though controversial, posed little threat of violence or illegal activity. Banks describes Cointelpro as one example of "executive misfeasance, a pattern of abuse that frequently battered civil rights and liberties under the pretext of making the nation secure."[75] In the most infamous example, the FBI secretly planted listening devices in the hotel room of civil rights leader Martin Luther King Jr. and, in an attempt to undermine his protest efforts, leaked some of the information obtained about his personal life.

The danger of unrestricted government spying is that it will be abused. In addition to violating the rights of dissidents such as King in the name of national security, government officials may use search and surveillance powers to further their own personal goals. The American public became aware of this danger through the Watergate scandal of the early 1970s, in which CIA agents used wiretaps and other intelligence tools against Democrats, antiwar protestors, and other political groups opposed to President Richard Nixon. The scandal forced Nixon's resignation and led to congressional hearings on the government's domestic intelligence operations.

A special committee led by Senator Frank Church (D-ID) investigated these intelligence abuses and found that nearly every modern president had authorized warrantless surveillance, often for political

purposes. The Church Committee's 1976 report recommended that Congress increase oversight of domestic intelligence operations and institute stricter regulations on how intelligence agencies share information with domestic law enforcement agencies such as the FBI. In response, Congress passed an array of legislation designed to curb government surveillance of U.S. citizens and protect individual privacy. Among these laws was the previously mentioned Foreign Intelligence Surveillance Act (FISA), the 1978 law that banned warrantless searches; created the secret FISA court to oversee intelligence operations; curtailed the CIA's domestic operations; and restricted information sharing between the CIA and the FBI. Through FISA and other reforms, the wall between intelligence gathering and law enforcement stood throughout the 1980s and 1990s.

Removing the Rules Against Information Sharing

After September 11, a consensus quickly emerged that this wall had hindered counterterrorism efforts and was a major factor in the FBI's failure to prevent the September 11 attacks. *Newsweek International* editor Fareed Zakaria argues that the FBI failed to discover the September 11 terrorists' plans because "no one at the FBI had the job of strategic analysis—i.e., of connecting the dots. . . . The FBI is a law-enforcement agency, not an intelligence outfit. To begin a massive operation, a crime

Tearing Down Walls

On April 14, 2004, FBI director Robert Mueller III gave a statement about the changes the FBI has made since September 11 before the National Commission on Terrorist Attacks upon the United States. Mueller emphasized the benefits of tearing down the walls between intelligence gathering and law enforcement.

The legal walls between intelligence and law enforcement operations that handicapped us before 9/11 have been eliminated. The PATRIOT Act, the Attorney General's intelligence sharing procedures and the opinion from the Foreign Intelligence Surveillance Court of Review tore down the legal impediments to coordination and information-sharing between criminal investigators and intelligence agents. We can now fully coordinate operations within the Bureau and with the Intelligence Community. We can also deploy the full range of investigative tools—both criminal processes like search warrants and needs to have been committed.

grand jury subpoenas and intelligence authorities like FISA wiretap warrants—to identify, investigate and neutralize terrorist threats. With these changes, we in the Bureau can finally take full operational advantage of our dual role as both a law enforcement and an intelligence agency.

We are eliminating the wall that historically stood between us and the CIA. The FBI and the CIA started exchanging senior personnel in 1996, and we have worked hard to build on that effort. Today, we and the CIA are integrated at virtually every level of our operations....

Removing these walls has been part of a comprehensive plan to strengthen the ability of the FBI to predict and prevent terrorism. We developed this plan immediately after the September 11th attacks....We have been steadily and methodically implementing it ever since.

needs to have been committed."[76] While the CIA and other intelligence organizations were monitoring suspected terrorists abroad, the reasoning goes, restrictions on domestic surveillance prevented the FBI from using wiretaps and other techniques to spy on possible terrorist individuals who were operating on U.S. soil.

In addition, the restrictions on information sharing between intelligence operations and criminal investigations prevented federal investigators from "connecting the dots" and discovering al Qaeda's plans. Testifying before Congress in 2003, U.S. attorney for the northern district of Illinois Patrick Fitzgerald explained his experience with restrictions on information sharing:

I was on a prosecution team in New York that began a criminal investigation of [al Qaeda leader] Usama Bin Laden in early 1996. The team—prosecutors and FBI agents assigned to the criminal case—had access to a number of sources. We could talk to citizens. We could talk to local police officers. We could talk to other U.S. government agencies. We could talk to foreign police officers.... But there was one group of people we were not permitted to talk to. Who? The FBI agents across the street from us in lower Manhattan assigned to a parallel intelligence investigation of Usama Bin Laden and al Qaeda. We could not learn what information they had gathered. That was "the wall."[77]

The DOJ, along with the Bush administration and many members of Congress, argued that the solution was to loosen the restrictions on information sharing. In his October 18, 2001, testimony urging passage of the Patriot Act, Ashcroft proclaimed that "tearing down the wall between intelligence and criminal information is one of the most important steps we will make or we will be able to take."[78] The specific provision of the Patriot Act that allows more information sharing among government agencies is Section 203. This section permits intelligence

CIA director Porter Goss and FBI director Robert Mueller convene during a meeting of the U.S. Senate Intelligence Committee. The Patriot Act allows for information to be shared between intelligence agents and criminal investigators.

information to be shared with any federal law enforcement official if it helps in the discharge of duties. In some cases, the Patriot Act requires the DOJ to inform the FISA Court, "within a reasonable time,"[79] of what intelligence information is shared, but in other cases no judicial review is required.

From a civil liberties perspective, the problem with information sharing is that it could provide investigators with a roundabout way to use antiterrorism powers in nonterrorism cases. In standard police investigations, information obtained illegally (through a warrantless search, for example) is usually inadmissible in court, and information sharing raises somewhat similar legal issues. In monitoring the communications of hundreds of suspected terrorists and the people they come in contact with, investigators are likely to learn of a large number of less serious, nonterrorist crimes. Without any restrictions on infor-

DEA agents in Miami escort Fabio Ochoa, a suspected cocaine smuggler, after he was extradited from Colombia in 2001. Agents from both the FBI and DEA investigated Ochoa.

mation sharing, investigators would be inclined to pass this information on to other agents investigating those types of crimes. For example, an FBI task force investigating terrorism might learn of a drug-smuggling operation and pass that information on to the DEA. In this way, the DEA investigators will have vicariously taken advantage of antiterrorism powers, and circumvented the Fourth Amendment's warrant requirements. Former attorney general Benjamin Civiletti had warned of this danger in 1979, in the context of information sharing between the FBI and CIA:

> You have to be extremely careful in working out, pursuant to the law, the information which is being exchanged, what its purpose is, how it was obtained and collected, so that you are not inadvertently ... corrupting the fact that the CIA's main duty is foreign intelligence, and they have no charter, no responsibility, ... no mission to investigate criminal acts in the United States.[80]

A Hybrid Organization

In addition to loosening the restrictions on information sharing, the other way that the Patriot Act lowers the wall between intelligence and law enforcement is by granting the FBI increased search and surveillance powers. In arguing for the Patriot Act, Senator Orrin Hatch (R-UT) explained, "Terrorists are a hybrid between domestic criminals and international agents. ... These hybrid criminals call for new hybrid tools."[81]

The Patriot Act has indeed made the FBI into a hybrid organization. On the one hand, it is a law enforcement agency, but it is also now charged with gathering intelligence in order to prevent terrorism, and under the Patriot Act it is less bound by Fourth Amendment restrictions than before. On the other hand, although the Patriot Act expands FBI agents' authority, they still operate on U.S. soil and are therefore more constrained by U.S. laws than, for example, CIA agents operating in the Middle East. Finally, unlike the CIA and other strictly intelligence-oriented organizations, the FBI is also responsible for dealing with "normal" criminals who do not pose a threat to national security.

In expanding the FBI's powers, the Patriot Act was the first major piece of legislation to address how the FBI should fulfill its role as an intelligence-gathering, terrorism-prevention agency. But the debate over the Patriot Act is complicated by the fact that many of its provisions also affect how it operates as a crime-solving law enforcement agency. By tearing down the wall between intelligence gathering and law enforcement, the Patriot Act changed the ways in which the FBI handles not just terrorism cases, but also normal criminal investigations.

The Patriot Act increases the FBI's intelligence-gathering powers by easing the restrictions on domestic surveillance contained in FISA. For example, Section 218 of the act empowers the FBI to obtain FISA warrants in investigations where intelligence gathering is a "significant purpose"[82]

63

of the investigation rather than the primary purpose. Critics of the law maintain that this change in wording is too vague, and could result in the FBI using FISA warrants in criminal cases that have little to do with terrorism. As former Clinton chief of staff John Podesta explains, "Section 218 is an important tool for counterterrorism but, since probable cause is not required under FISA, it also raises the possibility that U.S. citizens who are not terrorists could have their homes and belongings searched and communications monitored without probable cause."[83]

Moreover, the Patriot Act explicitly states that federal investigators may use some of the new search and surveillance powers in criminal investigations that have nothing to do with terrorism. For example, Section 213 authorizes sneak-and-peek searches in nonterrorist criminal investigations, and Section 216, which authorizes Internet surveillance, makes no requirement that such surveillance be used only in terrorism cases. According to critics of the Patriot Act, measures such as these show that the Patriot Act was a government power grab—that is, that the DOJ wanted the law to include the broadest search and surveillance powers it could get, not only to fight the war on terror, but to increase its power in general. "What the Justice Department has really done," says Elliot Mincberg, legal director of the liberal group People for the American Way, "is to get things put into the law that have been on prosecutors' wish lists for years. They've used terrorism as a guise to expand law

enforcement powers in areas that are totally unrelated to terrorism."[84]

The Patriot Act and Nonterrorist Crimes

Concerns about how the Patriot Act might be applied in nonterrorism cases are not just speculative. In its reports to Congress, the DOJ has cited cases in which Patriot Act provisions were used to investigate and prosecute a major drug trafficker, a four-time murderer, identity thieves, and a fugitive who used a fake passport in fleeing trial. Justice Department officials say that the cases cited in its reports to Congress represent only a small sampling of the hundreds of nonterrorism cases in which the Patriot Act has been implemented. The DOJ has adamantly defended these uses of the Patriot Act: "If it's good enough to be used against terrorists, it ought to be used against other kinds of criminals,"[85] says DOJ spokesman Mark Corallo.

But critics contend that the DOJ is applying the law in ways that Congress never intended. In 2003, for example, a twenty-year-old woman left two threatening notes in the bathroom of a cruise ship bound for Hawaii from Mexico, apparently because she wanted the ship to turn around so she could return to her boyfriend. Under the Patriot Act, threatening transportation facilities is a terrorist act, and the woman was sentenced to two years in prison. In another case, federal investigators used provisions of the Patriot Act to investigate Las Vegas strip club owners who were bribing politi-

Prior to passage of the Patriot Act, the Central Intelligence Agency (whose headquarters in Langley, Virginia, is pictured) was charged exclusively with gathering intelligence.

cians to loosen local regulations for the clubs. Civil liberties groups object to these uses of the Patriot Act that, as ACLU attorney Allen Lichtenstein puts it, "go far beyond reasonable national security needs."[86] Former representative Barr has expressed frustration that the Patriot Act has been used in criminal cases: "I took the administration at its word when it suggested the more wide-ranging powers in the law would be used exclusively for counter-terrorism, and were

only necessary given the extraordinary threat Al Qaeda and like groups represent. . . . Instead, however, the Bush administration has freely used the Patriot Act in cases unrelated to terrorism."[87]

Civil liberties groups argue that the curtailment of Fourth Amendment rights might be justified in terrorism cases, but that does not mean that they should be curtailed for all types of crimes. "Worries about terrorism provide no reason to expand law enforcement powers across the board,"[88] writes law professor Schulhofer. As Etzioni explains,

> It is well known that treating various kinds of offenses differently, according to their severity, is at the foundation of our legal and moral code. We do not condemn people to a lifetime in jail for jaywalking. According to the same code, we also calibrate the powers that we grant the government in dealing with suspects not yet convicted of anything.[89]

In this view, even though antiterrorism measures such as increased wiretap authority can help investigators prosecute all types of criminals, using the new powers so broadly would be excessive. And in Etzioni's opinion, doing so would be equivalent to "treating almost everybody as if they were suspected of terrorism."[90]

Dual Roles, Dual Concerns

These controversies over the search and surveillance powers the FBI should have, and the types of cases they should or should not use them in, ultimately hinge on the FBI's hybrid role in the war on terror. The agency still serves as a sort of federal police department, solving crimes and operating strictly as a law enforcement agency in the majority of its cases. But to fulfill its role in preventing terrorism, the FBI, using search and surveillance powers that the police gen-

---

The Exclusionary Rule

In the following excerpt from his book How Patriotic Is the Patriot Act? Freedom Versus Security in an Age of Terrorism, *Amitai Etzioni emphasizes how the warrant system helps ensure that law enforcement agents use their search and surveillance powers only when justified. In the following excerpt, Etzioni discusses the exclusionary rule, which ensures that only information collected with a warrant is allowable in court.*

In addition to the requirements that need to be met to get a warrant or court in the first place, courts ensure that law enforcement agents act within the limits of the power granted to them by suppressing evidence that is collected illegally. The exclu-sionary rule—that evidence collected in violation of the Fourth Amendment must be excluded from a trial against the suspect—was not originally written into the Constitution but was established in the Supreme Court case *Boyd v. United States.* . . . This serves not only to protect the suspect after a violation occurs but also to deter inappropriate searches because agents know that if they do not follow the correct procedures, the culprits might go free.

In Etzioni's view, information sharing among intelligence and law enforcement agencies could lead to violations of the exclusionary rule, if information obtained via special FISA warrants in terrorism cases is used to prosecute nonterrorism crimes.

---

erally do not have access to, also gathers intelligence on individuals who have not committed any crime.

In expanding the FBI's intelligence-gathering powers, the Patriot Act raises two separate concerns. First, there is the danger that the FBI might abuse its domestic surveillance powers by spying on Americans, as it did in the 1960s and 1970s. Second, there is the danger that search and surveillance powers intended to be used against terrorism might be used in criminal investigations where national security is not at stake.

Both dangers can be averted through the system of checks and balances on which the U.S. government is based. Electronic privacy advocate James X. Dempsey explains:

The choice is not between surveillance powers and no surveillance powers.

Civil libertarians engaged in the debate over the new terrorism laws do not argue that the government should be denied the tools it needs to monitor terrorists' communications. Instead, privacy advocates urge that those powers be focused and subject to clear standards and judicial review.[91]

In this view, congressional oversight of the DOJ and judicial oversight of individual FBI investigations can help ensure that the FBI fulfills its dual roles while also upholding civil liberties. As Zakaria argues, "There's only one way to get security and liberty at the same time. Authorize the FBI to engage in domestic intelligence with clearly demarcated powers; put the agency under much stronger 'civilian' surveillance, including from Congress; and let it know specifically what it can and cannot do."[92]

Chapter Five

The Ongoing Debate

When the Patriot Act was passed, just six weeks after the September 11 attacks, the nation was still caught up in waves of shock, mourning, fear, and anger. In addition, throughout October 2001, news stories about the Patriot Act (known simply as the Antiterrorism Act until shortly before it was passed) were overshadowed by two more dramatic developments. First, in Afghanistan, U.S. troops in Operation Enduring Freedom were on the hunt for Osama bin Laden and other al Qaeda leaders. Second, on the home front, the United States seemed to be facing a possible new terrorist threat in the form of anthrax. Throughout October and into November, anonymous individuals mailed anthrax spores to several media outlets and to Congress, infecting dozens of people with the potentially lethal disease.

In this atmosphere, many Americans were much more concerned with safety than with how the Patriot Act might affect civil liberties. Organizations such as the ACLU, the Center for Constitutional Rights (CCR), and the Electronic Privacy Information Center (EPIC) were protesting the law, but public opinion was firmly behind the new antiterror measures: An ABC News poll conducted late in September found that 92 percent of Americans supported new laws that would make it easier for the government to catch terrorists.

Signs of a Backlash

As time went on, however, public opinion grew more ambivalent, as people expressed more concern about privacy and other civil liberties. "In the immediate aftermath of Sept. 11, two out of three Americans said some civil liberties had to be given up to fight terrorism," wrote *Boston Globe* reporter Charlie Savage in October 2004, "but a recent Pew Foundation poll indicated that half as many Americans now hold that view."[93] While polls show that a majority of Americans—about 53 to 56 percent—support the Patriot Act, an April 2004 Fox News poll found that 28 percent of respondents felt that the law "goes too far and could violate the civil liberties of average Americans."[94]

The clearest evidence of a backlash against the Patriot Act is the growing number of towns, cities, counties, and states that have passed resolutions opposing the law.

One week after the September 11 attacks, two policemen in New York's financial district stand guard next to a wanted poster of Osama bin Laden.

The resolution passed by the city of Providence, Rhode Island, is typical:

> The USA Patriot Act . . . weakens, contradicts and undermines [Americans'] basic constitutional rights. . . . The Providence City Council calls on our United States Representatives and Senators to . . . actively work for the repeal of the Act or those sections of the Act . . . that violate fundamental rights and liberties as stated in the United States Constitution and its Amendments.[95]

In 2002, just 22 communities passed anti–Patriot Act resolutions such as these. However, in 2003, 218 communities, including the state governments of Vermont, Alaska, and Hawaii, passed such resolutions, and 130 more, including the state government of Maine, followed suit in 2004.

One reason the Patriot Act has become such a source of controversy is that, as journalist Vanessa Blum explains, "The law has become a lightning rod for an array of concerns, including some not directly related to the Patriot Act."[96] Debate over the Patri-

The ACLU's Influence

With its "Keep America Safe and Free" campaign, the American Civil Liberties Union has played a significant role in raising public concern about the Patriot Act. Many of the 370 cities, towns, counties, and states that have passed resolutions protesting the Patriot Act did so at the prompting of ACLU members. The ACLU Web site encourages concerned citizens to promote such resolutions, and provides a "Model Local Resolution to Protect Civil Liberties," excerpted here:

WHEREAS federal policies adopted since September 11, 2001, including provisions in the USA PATRIOT Act (Public Law 107-56) and related executive orders, regulations and actions threaten fundamental rights and liberties. . . .

THEREFORE BE IT RESOLVED THAT THE COUNCIL OF THE CITY OF _____:

1. AFFIRMS its strong support for fundamental constitutional rights and its opposition to federal measures that infringe on civil liberties. . . .

6. DIRECTS the City Council Chief of Staff to:

a. Transmit a copy of this resolution to Senators _____ and _____, and Representatives _____ accompanied by a letter urging them to:

• support Congressional efforts to assess the impacts of the PATRIOT Act

• monitor federal anti-terrorism tactics and work to repeal provisions of the USA PATRIOT ACT and other laws and regulations that infringe on civil rights and liberties

• ensure that provisions of the USA PATRIOT Act "sunset" in accordance with the provisions of the Act

ot Act is often tied up with a wide variety of other civil liberties issues, including the government's detention of hundreds of immigrants in the days after September 11; the continuing imprisonment, without trial, of hundreds of terror suspects at the U.S. naval base at Guantánamo Bay, Cuba; Bush's November 13, 2001, executive order authorizing the use of military tribunals to try terrorism suspects; the Department of Defense's Total Information Awareness project, which aims to connect all the information that state and federal government agencies have on individual citizens into one massive database; and the creation of the previously mentioned Department of Homeland Security in March 2003. Protest of these issues often includes opposition to the Patriot Act, to the point that protesting the Patriot Act has become a way to raise general awareness about how the war on terror is affecting civil liberties. As Timothy Lynch of the libertarian Cato Institute puts it, "The law has taken on symbolic proportions over and above the nitty-gritty impact of its actual provisions."[97]

Legislative Action

When civil liberties groups do discuss the specifics of the Patriot Act, they tend to focus on Section 215, which authorizes the attorney general to search an individual's private records without the target's knowledge. Although the Patriot Act does not specify what types of records may be searched, civil liberties groups point out that the government might search an indi-

vidual's library records, or force a bookseller to reveal a customer's purchases. The specter of the government monitoring what people read was enough to prompt several members of Congress to try to repeal Section 215 in 2003. In the House, Representative Bernard Sanders (I-VT) proposed the Freedom to Read Protection Act, while in the Senate, Lisa Murkowski (R-AL) and Ron Wyden (D-OR) introduced the Protecting the Rights of Individuals Act and Russ Feingold (D-WI) sponsored the Library, Bookseller, and Personal Records Privacy Act. All three bills sought to weaken or repeal Section 215, but none of them was passed by either branch of Congress.

Another of the most controversial sections of the Patriot Act has been Section 213, which authorizes sneak-and-peek searches. In summer 2003, Congressman "Butch" Otter (R-ID), one of only three House Republicans to vote against the Patriot Act, introduced a bill that would eliminate funding for searches under Section 213. The "Otter Amendment" passed overwhelmingly in the House, but the Senate refused to take up the bill.

The Bush Administration Responds

In response to civil libertarians' criticisms, shifting public opinion, and congressional attempts to weaken the law, the Bush administration initiated a public relations campaign in support of the Patriot Act. Government officials have made the case for the Patriot Act with three main points.

First, they maintain that the law allows federal investigators more easily to use important tools—such as roving wiretaps and sneak-and-peek searches—in terrorism cases. The DOJ maintains that these methods were previously available to law enforcement in organized crime cases. Second, they emphasize that the Patriot Act facilitates information sharing among law enforcement and intelligence agencies so they can better "connect the dots." Third, they argue the Patriot Act updates wiretap law to deal with modern communications technologies.

In addition, DOJ officials cite the arrests that have been made in the war on terror. Speaking in November 2003, Ashcroft said that

> the Patriot Act has enabled us to make quiet, steady progress in the war on terror. Since September 11, we have dismantled terrorist cells in Detroit, Seattle, Portland, Tampa, Northern Virginia, and Buffalo. We have disrupted weapons procurement plots in Miami, San Diego, Newark, and Houston. We have shut down terrorist-affiliated charities in Chicago, Dallas and Syracuse. We have brought criminal charges against 286 individuals. We have secured convictions or guilty pleas from 155 people.[98]

Above all, Ashcroft and other supporters of the Patriot Act have reminded Americans that there has not been a major terrorist attack on U.S. soil since the Patriot Act was passed. "American freedom has been enhanced, not diminished," says Ashcroft. "The Constitution has been honored, not degraded."[99]

In the summer of 2003—partly in response to the House's passage of the Otter Amendment—the DOJ launched a Web site to elaborate on these themes. The site's motto, "Preserving Life and Liberty," is perhaps an answer to the ACLU's slogan for its anti–Patriot Act campaign, "Keeping America Safe and Free." The lifeandliberty.gov site contains speeches and editorials supporting the Patriot Act, as well as a section devoted to "dispelling the myths" about the law.

To coincide with the launching of life andliberty.gov, Ashcroft went on a nationwide, thirty-two-city speaking tour to defend the Patriot Act. Former deputy assistant attorney general Dinh explained that the purpose of the tour was to "correct the misperceptions that are out there and to disabuse the American public of the misinformation they've gotten."[100] In his first speech of the tour, Ashcroft once again reiterated the DOJ's three arguments for the Patriot Act, concluding that "if we knew then what we know now, we would have passed the Patriot Act six months before September 11th rather than six weeks after the attacks."[101]

Patriot II

The Bush administration has also argued that even broader law enforcement powers may be necessary for the war on terror. The

Peaceful demonstrators in New York City protest John Ashcroft's 2003 speaking tour.

discussion about a possible sequel to the Patriot Act has come in two separate phases. First, in early 2003 a DOJ draft of a sequel to the Patriot Act was leaked to the media. Then, in fall 2003, Bush began arguing for several expansions of the Patriot Act.

In February 2003, an anonymous source sent a DOJ draft of a bill entitled the Domestic Security Enhancement Act to the Center for Public Integrity, a nonpartisan journalists' organization. The bill—quickly dubbed "Patriot II" in the media—would expand the government's antiterrorism powers by amending FISA and the Patriot Act itself. For example,

Patriot II would further loosen restrictions on the use of wiretaps; further increase the attorney general's authority to deport immigrants; make it easier for federal, state, and local law enforcement agencies to share information; and allow the death penalty for many terrorist crimes. Perhaps most controversially, the law would allow the government to keep terrorism arrests a secret, negating a previous federal court ruling that forced the DOJ to disclose the names of individuals detained after September 11.

Given the growing criticism of the Patriot Act at the time, writes Ball, "the draft did not have a very receptive audience."[102]

In fact, to individuals and groups who were already protesting the Patriot Act, Patriot II was an outrage. Journalist Robyn Blumner expressed a view common among civil libertarians: "Patriot II would only embolden the get-out-of-my-face arrogance of the Justice Department."[103] The DOJ declined to comment on the leaked draft, and when Ashcroft went on his speaking tour to

defend the Patriot Act a few months later, he made little mention of expanding the law.

But then, in a September 10, 2003, speech before U.S. Marine troops and FBI agents in Quantico, Virginia, Bush revisited the idea of Patriot II:

The Patriot Act imposed tough new penalties on terrorists and those who

Soldiers escort a detainee into the maximum security prison camp at Guantánamo Bay. Under "Patriot II," the government would be able to secretly arrest suspected terrorists.

support them. But as the fight against terrorists progressed, we have found areas where more help is required. Under current federal law, there are unreasonable obstacles to investigating and prosecuting terrorism, obstacles that don't exist when law enforcement officials are going after embezzlers or drug traffickers. For the sake of the American people, Congress should change the law, and give law enforcement officials the same tools they have to fight terror that they have to fight other crime.[104]

In the speech, Bush proposed three enhancements to the Patriot Act. First, he spoke of the need to give administrative subpoena authority to the FBI, which would allow FBI agents to demand documents or testimony from individuals without court approval. Second, Bush argued that terrorism suspects should be held without bail. Finally, the president argued that more terrorist crimes should qualify for capital punishment. Bush repeated his call to expand the Patriot Act in speeches throughout 2004, asserting that "the Patriot Act needs to be renewed and the Patriot Act needs to be enhanced."[105]

The Bush administration has thus answered the critics of the Patriot Act not just by defending the law, but by arguing that it should be strengthened. Former Senate counsel Beryl Howell, who participated in the negotiations over the Patriot Act, describes the strategy this way: "The best defense is a good offense. . . . Their attitude

is 'if you think the USA Patriot Act is so bad, wait and see what else we want.'"[106] Kettl describes the Bush administration's call to expand the Patriot Act "a particularly tough tactic to fight rising efforts in Congress and across the country to repeal portions of the USA Patriot Act."[107]

Sunset, Renew, or Amend?

However, before Congress considers expanding the Patriot Act, it will have to decide whether or not to renew the provisions of the law that are set to expire at the end of 2005. These sections include part of Section 203, which allows the sharing, without judicial review, of information gained from wiretaps and other intelligence-gathering techniques; Section 206, which authorizes roving wiretaps; Section 214, which loosens restrictions on the use of pen register and trap-and-trace wiretaps; Section 218, which allows FISA warrants when foreign intelligence is a "significant" rather than the primary purpose of an investigation; Section 220, which authorizes "nationwide" warrants; and Section 215, which empowers the attorney general to search an individual's private records.

Bush has made his stance on renewal clear: "We must not allow the passage of time or the illusion of safety to weaken our resolve in this new war," he said in a March 2005 speech. "To protect the American people, Congress must promptly renew all provisions of the Patriot Act this year."[108] Gonzales has echoed the president's resolve, stating that the Patriot Act has made the nation safer and that "there has not been one verified civil rights abuse under the Patriot Act."[109] DOJ officials also maintain that Congress should not merely renew the temporary provisions of the Patriot Act, but also make them permanent.

A few civil liberties groups argue that all of the sunset provisions of the Patriot Act should be allowed to expire. In 2004, for example, the Electronic Frontier Foundation launched a "Let the Sun Set on the Patriot Act" campaign, profiling each one of the provisions scheduled to sunset and explaining why it believes Congress should not renew it.

However, a more common view among critics of the law is Congress should not simply decide between renewing the Patriot Act or allowing some of its provisions to expire. Instead, groups such as the Center for Democracy and Technology maintain that Congress should use the sunset debate to take an in-depth look at the Patriot Act and revise the law to address civil libertarians' concerns: "Many of even the controversial provisions that are due to sunset

The Debate over Administrative Subpoenas

One of the measures that President Bush has said he would like to see Congress grant to the FBI is administrative subpoena authority. A subpoena is a government document, normally issued by a court, that orders an individual to turn over evidence or give testimony. An administrative subpoena is a subpoena issued by an officer of the executive branch—such as an FBI agent.

The FBI already has broad authority to request grand jury, or court-ordered, subpoenas in terrorism cases. In a June 22, 2004, Senate Judiciary Committee hearing on the subject, Senator Patrick Leahy argued that administrative subpoenas are unnecessary: "I hope the [administration] will explain why grand jury subpoenas, which are available in terrorism cases, are not adequate government power and individual agents need to wield administrative authority without supervision."

In an April 20, 2004, speech, President Bush argued that using administrative subpoenas "speeds up the process whereby people can gain information to go after terrorists." Administrative subpoenas can be obtained nearly instantaneously, whereas grand jury subpoenas may take hours or days. At the June 2004 Senate hearing, Assistant Attorney General Rachel Brand also emphasized speed, describing a hypothetical scenario in which the extra time saved by using an administrative rather than a grand jury subpoena would save lives.

The emerging controversy over administrative subpoenas is yet another example of how national security measures, which prize speed and efficiency, often conflict with civil liberties, which rely on a sometimes time-consuming system of checks and balances.

should not expire entirely. Instead, the sunset debate should focus on amending the Act to include the checks and balances that were left out in the haste to enact the law. Keep the tools, but make sure they are under control."[110]

One reason why most civil liberties groups do not favor simply allowing the sunset provisions of the Patriot Act to expire is that some of the most controversial provisions of the law are *not* set to expire. These include part of Section 203, which allows the sharing of some types of intelligence information without judicial review; Section 213, which authorizes sneak-and-peek searches; Section 216, which states that pen register wiretaps may be used for Internet surveillance; Section 505, which empowers the attorney general to issue national security letters in any type of investigation;

President Bush believes that the FBI should have the power to issue administrative subpoenas.

and Section 802, which provides a broad definition of "domestic terrorism." Critics of the Patriot Act see the sunset debate as an opportunity to reopen debate on these provisions as well as those set to expire.

One group advocating for this type of debate is the Patriots to Restore Checks and Balances. Led by Republican former representative Barr, Patriots is actually an alliance of groups that includes the ACLU as well as

conservative organizations—such as the Eagle Forum and the Gun Owners of America—that usually side with the Bush administration on most issues. In its mission statement, the alliance states that

Congress must resist the current push to make permanent the expiring provisions in the . . . USA Patriot Act, and should deliberate at length before deciding whether to reauthorize any of the "sunseted" provisions in the law. Our lawmakers should also fix other provisions of the Patriot Act, including those authorizing secret search warrants and an overbroad definition of domestic terrorism. . . . Congress should use the debate about the sunsets as a springboard into a broader conversation about the health of checks and balances post-9/11.[111]

"Our goal is not to gut the Patriot Act," said Barr in March 2005, but rather to push for debate over "the single most important issue that will be facing this country over the next two years."[112]

A Symbol of the War on Terror

One piece of proposed legislation that has drawn considerable attention during the sunset debate is the Security and Freedom Ensured (SAFE) Act, which would require stricter judicial review of many search and surveillance powers, such as sneak-and-peek searches and roving wiretaps. "I believe it is possible to combat terrorism and preserve our individual freedoms at

A man tapes his mouth shut in protest of the Patriot Act during the Democratic National Convention in 2004.

FBI agents remove boxes of evidence during a 2002 raid on a New York home of five suspected al Qaeda members.

the same time," said Senator Dick Durbin (D-IL), a cosponsor of the SAFE Act. "The PATRIOT Act crossed the line on several key areas of civil liberties, and this legislation restores the necessary checks and balances to the system."[113] However, the DOJ strongly opposes the law: According to Ashcroft, "If enacted, the SAFE Act would roll back many of the most useful and important anti-terrorism authorities enacted by the USA PATRIOT Act. In fact, the SAFE Act would make it even more difficult to mount an effective anti-terror campaign than it was before the PATRIOT Act was passed."[114]

These comments on the SAFE Act and the sunset provisions of the Patriot Act show just how sharp the division is between supporters and critics of the Patriot Act. Dis-

cussing renewal of the Patriot Act in March 2005, Senator John Cornyn (R-TX) stated simply that "this is going to provoke a lot of debate."[115] That may be a significant understatement. The Patriot Act has come to symbolize the larger debate over how the United States should approach the war on terror. On the one hand, the government wants to appear tough and uncompromising on terrorism, and so the Bush administration has been tough and uncompromising on the Patriot Act. On the other hand, to critics of the law, the Patriot Act has become a symbol of the government's apparent willingness to put concerns about national security ahead of civil liberties. Passed so quickly in the weeks after September 11, the Patriot Act will likely be a source of controversy for decades to come.

Notes

Introduction: A Question of Balance

1. Roger Dean Golden, "What Price Security? The USA PATRIOT Act and America's Balance Between Freedom and Security," in Michael W. Ritz, Ralph G. Hensley Jr., and James C. Whitmire, eds., *The Homeland Security Papers: Stemming the Tide of Terror*, Maxwell Air Force Base, AL: USAF Counterproliferation Center, February 2004, p. 6.
2. Golden, "What Price Security?" p. 9.
3. American Civil Liberties Union, *Insatiable Appetite: The Government's Demand for New and Unnecessary Powers After September 11*, April 2002. www.aclu.org/Files/OpenFile.cfm?id=14799.
4. Quoted in Howard Ball, *The USA Patriot Act: Balancing Civil Liberties and National Security: A Reference Handbook*, Santa Barbara, CA: ABC-CLIO, 2004, p. 47.
5. American Civil Liberties Union, *Civil Liberties After 9/11: The ACLU Defends Freedom*. www.aclu.org/SafeandFree/SafiendFree.cfm?ID=108988&c=207.
6. Quoted in Michael Duffy and Nancy Gibbs, "How Far Do We Want the FBI to Go?" *Time*, June 10, 2002, p. 24.
7. Dan Collins, testimony before the Senate Judiciary Committee, September 22, 2004. http://judiciary.senate.gov/testimony.cfm?id=1312.
8. Quoted in Ball, *The USA Patriot Act*, p. 48.
9. Quoted in Golden, "What Price Security," p. 19.
10. Jay Winik, "Security Before Liberty: Today's Curbs on Freedom Are Nothing Compared with Earlier Wars," *OpinionJournal*, October 23, 2001. www.opinionjournal.com/editorial/feature.html.
11. John Ashcroft, testimony before the House Committee on the Judiciary, September 24, 2001. www.usdoj.gov/archive/ag/testimony/2001/agcrisisremarks9_24.htm.
12. Ashcroft, testimony before the House Committee on the Judiciary, September 24, 2001.
13. Heather MacDonald, "Straight Talk on Homeland Security," *City Journal*, vol. 13, no. 3, Summer 2003. www.city-journal.org/html/13_3_straight_talk.html.
14. Jay Stanley and Barry Steinhardt, *Bigger Monster, Weaker Chains: The Growth of the American Surveillance Society*, New York: ACLU, January 2003. www.aclu.org/Privacy/Privacy.cfm?ID=11572.
15. Stanley and Steinhardt, *Bigger Monster, Weaker Chains*.
16. Donald F. Kettl, *System Under Stress: Homeland Security and American Politics*, Washington, DC: CQ Press, 2004, p. 111.

Chapter 1: The Passage of the Patriot Act and Its Key Provisions

17. Robert O'Harrow, "Six Weeks in Autumn," *Washington Post*, October 27, 2002, p. W06.
18. John Ashcroft, remarks before U.S.

Mayors Conference, October 25, 2001. www.usdoj.gov/archive/ag/speeches/2001/agcrisisremarks10_25.htm.

19. Quoted in O'Harrow, "Six Weeks in Autumn," p. W06.

20. Steven Brill, *After: The Rebuilding and Defending of America in the September 12 Era*, New York: Simon & Schuster, 2003, p. 74.

21. Quoted in Brill, *After*, p. 18.

22. Coalition in Defense of Freedom, "In Defense of Freedom at a Time of Crisis," September 18, 2001. www.americanhumanist.org/press/coalition.html.

23. O'Harrow, "Six Weeks in Autumn," p. W06.

24. Quoted in Ball, *The USA Patriot Act*, p. 46.

25. Ashcroft, testimony before the House Committee on the Judiciary, September 24, 2001.

26. Quoted in Christopher P. Banks, "Protecting (or Destroying) Freedom Through Law: The USA PATRIOT Act's Constitutional Implications," in David B. Cohen and John W. Wells, eds., *American National Security and Civil Liberties in an Era of Terrorism*, New York: Palgrave Macmillan, 2004, p. 30.

27. USA Patriot Act, H.R. 3162, October 24, 2001, p. 155.www.findlaw.com.

28. George W. Bush, "President Signs Anti-Terrorism Bill," October 26, 2001. www.whitehouse.gov/news/releases/2001/10/.

29. Ashcroft, remarks before U.S. Mayors Conference, October 25, 2001.

30. Ashcroft, remarks before U.S. Mayors Conference, October 25, 2001.

31. Kettl, *System Under Stress*, p. 97.

32. Quoted in Frank Viviano, "Organized Crime Said to Launder Billions for Terrorists," *San Francisco Chronicle*, September 23, 2001, p. A12.

33. Kettl, *System Under Stress*, p. 97.

34. Ann McFeatters and Karen MacPherson, "Patriot Act May See Revisions," *Pittsburgh Post-Gazette*, April 26, 2004, p. A1.

Chapter 2: Expanded Surveillance Powers and the Fourth Amendment

35. Stephen J. Scholhofer, "No Checks, No Balances," in Richard C. Leone and Greg Anrig Jr., eds., *The War on Our Freedoms: Civil Liberties in an Age of Terrorism*, New York: PublicAffairs, 2003, p. 79.

36. Banks, "Protecting (or Destroying) Freedom Through Law," p. 36.

37. Mark Reibling, "Uncuff the FBI," *OpinionJournal*, June 4, 2002. www.opinionjournal.com/editorial/feature.html.

38. FindLaw for Legal Professionals, *United States v. United States District Court*, 407 U.S. 297 (1972). http://laws.findlaw.com/us/407/297.html.

39. John Ashcroft, press conference, October 18, 2001. www.usdoj.gov/archive/ag/speeches/2001/agcrisisremarks10_18.htm.

40. Dahlia Lithwick and Julia Turner, "A Guide to the Patriot Act, Part 2," *Slate*, September 10, 2003. http://slate.msn.com/id/2088106/.

41. Alice Fisher, testimony before the Senate Judiciary Committee, October 9, 2002. http://judiciary.senate.gov/testimony.cfm?id=495&wit_id=1249.

42. Electronic Frontier Foundation, "FOIA Request to DOJ Concerning Pen-Trap Surveillance," January 13, 2005. www.eff.org/news/archives/2005_01.php.

43. Fisher, testimony before the Senate Judiciary Committee.

44. USA Patriot Act of 2001, Public Law 107-56, *U.S. Statutes at Large* 115 (2001), Sec. 220.

45. Stanley and Steinhardt, *Bigger Monster, Weaker Chains.*

46. U.S. Department of Justice, "Dispelling the Myths," Preserving Life & Liberty. www.lifeandliberty.gov/subs/u_myths. htm.

47. American Civil Liberties Union, *Unpatriotic Acts: The FBI's Power to Rifle Through Your Records and Personal Belongings Without Telling You.* New York: ACLU, July 2003. www.aclu. org/Files/OpenFile.cfm?id=13245.

48. Amitai Etzioni, *How Patriotic Is the Patriot Act? Freedom Versus Security in an Age of Terrorism*, New York: Routledge, 2004, p. 4.

Chapter 3: First Amendment and Immigrant Rights

49. Quoted in Matthew Rothschild, "The New McCarthyism," *Progressive*, January 2002. https://secure.progressive. org/0901/roth0102.html.

50. American Library Association, "Resolution on the Patriot Act," January 29, 2003. www.ala.org/Template.cfm?Section=ifresolutions&Template=/ContentManagement/Cor.

51. Quoted in David Mehegan, "Literary Groups Decry Patriot Act as Invasion of Privacy," *Boston Globe*, May 16, 2003, p. A6.

52. *San Francisco Chronicle*, "Privacy and Security; A Librarian's Dilemma," February 2, 2003, p. D4.

53. Robin Rice, "The USA Patriot Act and American Libraries," *Information for Social Change*, Winter 2002/2003. www. libr.org/ISC/articles/16-Rice.html.

54. American Civil Liberties Union, "Section 215 FAQ," October 24, 2002. www.aclu.org/Privacy/Privacy.cfm?ID=11054&c=130.

55. James D. Zirin, "Fearful Patriot Act?" *Washington Times*, October 22, 2004, p. A18.

56. John Ashcroft, "The Proven Tactics in the Fight Against Crime," Washington, DC, September 15, 2003. www.usdoj. gov/archive/ag/speeches/2003/091503 nationalrestaurant.htm.

57. USA Patriot Act, Sec. 215.

58. Quoted in Dahlia Lithwick and Julia Turner, "A Guide to the Patriot Act, Part 1," *Slate*, September 8, 2003. http:// slate.msn.com/id/2087984/.

59. USA Patriot Act, Sec. 802.

60. Nancy Chang, *The USA Patriot Act: What's So Patriotic About Trampling the Bill of Rights?* Center for Constitutional Rights, November 2001. www.ccr-ny. org/2/reports/docs/USA_PATRIOT_ ACT.pdf.

61. Quoted in Kevin Galvin, "Rights and Wrongs," *Seattle Times*, December 6, 2001, p. A6.

62. U.S. Department of Justice, "Dispelling the Myths."

63. Dahlia Lithwick and Julia Turner, "A Guide to the Patriot Act, Part 4," *Slate*, September 11, 2003. http://slate.msn. com/id/2088239/.

64. Quoted in Ruth Rosen, "Could It Happen Again?" *San Francisco Chronicle*, May 12, 2003. www.commondreams. org/views03/0512-01.htm.

65. USA Patriot Act, Sec. 411.

66. American Civil Liberties Union, "How the Anti-Terrorism Bill Allows for

Detention of People Engaging in Innocent Associational Activity," October 23, 2001. www.aclu.org/NationalSecurity/NationalSecurity.cfm?ID=9152&c=111.

67. Center for Constitutional Rights, *The State of Civil Liberties: One Year Later*, September 2002. www.ccr-ny.org.

68. Richard Lamm, "Terrorism and Immigration: We Need a Border," *Vital Speeches of the Day*, March 1, 2002, p. 298.

69. USA Patriot Act, Sec. 412.

70. Chang, *The USA Patriot Act.*

Chapter 4:
The Changing Role of the FBI

71. Etzioni, *How Patriotic Is the Patriot Act?*, p. 4.

72. Alberto Gonzales, remarks before the National Association of Counties Legislative Conference, Washington, DC, March 7, 2005. www.usdoj.gov/ag/speeches/2005/03072005_naco.htm.

73. Duffy and Gibbs, "How Far Do We Want the FBI to Go?" p. 24.

74. Quoted in Select Committee to Study Government Operations with Respect to Intelligence Activities, *Intelligence Activities and the Rights of Americans, Book II*, April 26, 1976. www.icdc.com/~paulwolf/cointelpro/churchfinalreport//ca.htm.

75. Banks, "Protecting (or Destroying) Freedom Through Law", p. 32.

76. Fareed Zakaria, "The Answer? A Domestic CIA," *Newsweek*, May 27, 2002, p. 39.

77. Patrick J. Fitzgerald, testimony before the Senate Judiciary Committee, October 21, 2003. http://judiciary.senate.gov/testimony.cfm?id=1439&wit_id=3936.

78. Ashcroft, press conference, October 18, 2001.

79. USA Patriot Act, Sec. 203.

80. Quoted in Patrick Leahy, statement on the passage of the Patriot Act, October 25, 2001. http://leahy.senate.gov/issues/targetterror/.

81. Quoted in Jim McGee, "An Intelligence Giant in the Making," *Washington Post*, November 4, 2001, p. 4.

82. USA Patriot Act, Sec. 208.

83. John Podesta, "USA Patriot Act: The Good, the Bad, and the Sunset," *Human Rights*, Winter 2002. www.abanet.org/irr/hr/winter02/podesta.html.

84. Quoted in Eric Lichtblau, "U.S. Uses Terror Law to Pursue Crimes from Drugs to Swindling," *New York Times*, September 28, 2003, p. 1.

85. Quoted in Sam Stanton and Emily Bazar, "Patriot Act's Broad Brush," *Sacramento Bee*, December 21, 2003, p. A1.

86. Quoted in Steve Friess, "Patriot Act Gets Mixed Reviews in Vegas," *Boston Globe*, November 8, 2003, p. A3.

87. Bob Barr, testimony before the Senate Judiciary Committee, September 22, 2004. http://judiciary.senate.gov/testimony.cfm?id=1312&wit_id=2874.

88. Stephen J. Scholhofer, "No Checks, No Balances," p. 79.

89. Etzioni, *How Patriotic Is the Patriot Act?* p. 30.

90. Etzioni, *How Patriotic Is the Patriot Act?*, p. 30.

91. James X. Dempsey, "Civil Liberties in a Time of Crisis." Winter 2002. www.abanet.org.irr/hr/winter02/dempsey.html.

92. Zakaria, "The Answer? A Domestic CIA," p. 39.

Chapter 5: The Ongoing Debate

93. Charlie Savage, "Civil-Liberties Issue in the Background," *Boston Globe*, October 4, 2004, p. A6.

94. Quoted in Pollingreport.com, "War on Terrorism."

95. Quoted in American Civil Liberties Union, "List of Communities That Have Passed Resolutions." www.aclu.org/SafeandFree/.

96. Vanessa Blum, "Pitching the Patriot Act," *Legal Times*, August 2, 2004.

97. Quoted in Blum, "Pitching the Patriot Act."

98. John Ashcroft, remarks before the Federalist Society National Convention, November 15, 2003. www.lifeandliberty.gov/subs/speeches/agspeechfeder.htm.

99. Ashcroft, remarks before the Federalist Society National Convention, November 15, 2003.

100. Quoted in Eric Lichtblau, "Administration Plans Defense of Terror Law," *New York Times*, August 19, 2003, p. A1.

101. John Ashcroft, speech before the American Enterprise Institute, August 19, 2003. www.aei.org/publications/pubID.19040,filter.all/.

102. Ball, *The USA Patriot Act*, p. 119.

103. Robyn E. Blumner, "If You Liked Patriot I, Don't Miss the Sequel," *St. Petersburg Times*, February 16, 2003, p. 1D.

104. George W. Bush, remarks before the FBI Academy, Quantico, VA, September 10, 2003. www.whitehouse.gov/news/releases/2003/09/images/20030910-6-quantico2-d-pm-0910-515h.html.

105. George W. Bush, remarks at Kleinshans Music Hall, Buffalo, NY, April 20, 2004. www.whitehouse.gov/news/releases/2004/04/20040420.

106. Quoted in Ball, *The USA Patriot Act*, p. 129.

107. Kettl, *System Under Stress*, p. 106.

108. Quoted in Bob Dart, "Patriot Act Faces Opposition from the Left and Right," *San Diego Union-Tribune*, March 23, 2005.

109. Quoted in Dart, "Patriot Act Faces Opposition from the Left and Right."

110. Center for Democracy and Technology, "Patriot Act Sunsets," May 7, 2004. www.cdt.org/security/usapatriot/analysis.shtml.

111. Patriots to Restore Checks and Balances. www.checksbalances.org.

112. Quoted in Dart, "Patriot Act Faces Opposition from the Left and Right."

113. Quoted in Dick Durbin, "Bipartisan Group of Senators Unveil 'Safe Act,'" October 15, 2003. http:// durbin.senate.gov.

114. John Ashcroft, letter to Senator Orrin Hatch, January 28, 2004. www.cdt.org.

115. Quoted in Chuck McCutcheon, "Dispute Looms on Patriot Act Renewals," *Times-Picayune*, March 23, 2005, p. 4.

For Further Reading

Web Sites

American Civil Liberties Union (ACLU)
(www.aclu.org). This national organization defends Americans' civil rights as guaranteed in the U.S. Constitution. Its Web site offers numerous reports, fact sheets, and policy statements on the Patriot Act, government surveillance, and homeland security measures targeted at immigrants.

ANSER Institute for Homeland Security
(www.homelandsecurity.org). This nonprofit, nonpartisan think tank works to educate the public about homeland security issues. The institute's Web site contains a virtual library of fact sheets, reports, legislation, and government documents and statistics on homeland security issues.

Center for Constitutional Rights (CCR)
(www.ccr-ny.org). Dedicated to protecting and advancing the rights guaranteed by the U.S. Constitution, this organization opposes many of the measures in the Patriot Act. A variety of fact sheets and reports are available on its Web site.

Department of Homeland Security (DHS)
(www.dhs.gov). This Web site offers a wide variety of information on homeland security, including press releases, speeches and testimony, and reports on new initiatives in the war on terrorism.

Electronic Privacy Information Center (EPIC) (www.epic.org/privacy/terrorism). A public interest research center that focuses on privacy and the First Amendment, EPIC maintains that the Patriot Act undermines key civil liberties. Its Web site contains numerous reports and fact sheets on the law.

National Immigration Forum (NIF)
(www.immigrationforum.org). This organization advocates public policies that welcome immigrants and refugees and that are fair and supportive to newcomers to the United States. The NIF Web site offers a special section on immigration in the wake of September 11.

Preserving Life & Liberty (www.lifeandliberty. gov). Set up by the U.S. Department of Justice to address civil libertarians' concerns about the Patriot Act and other homeland security initiatives, this Web site offers answers to frequently asked questions about the Patriot Act and testimony from U.S. officials in support of the act.

Works Consulted

Books

Howard Ball, *The USA Patriot Act: Balancing Civil Liberties and National Security: A Reference Handbook.* Santa Barbara, CA: ABC-CLIO, 2004. Ball provides a comprehensive overview of the issues surrounding the Patriot Act as well as other laws, passed before and after the Patriot Act, that have impacted both the war on terrorism and civil liberties.

Steven Brill, *After: The Rebuilding and Defending of America in the September 12 Era.* New York: Simon & Schuster, 2003. Brill offers a detailed, day-by-day chronicle of how the Bush administration responded to September 11. The first two hundred pages of the book cover the negotiations over the Patriot Act.

David B. Cohen and John W. Wells, eds., *American National Security and Civil Liberties in an Era of Terrorism.* New York: Palgrave Macmillan, 2004. This anthology's eleven essays examine how the war on terror is affecting civil liberties. One essay focuses entirely on the Patriot Act.

Amitai Etzioni, *How Patriotic Is the Patriot Act? Freedom Versus Security in an Age of Terrorism.* New York: Routledge, 2004. Etzioni assesses a variety of national security measures, beyond those included in the Patriot Act, and in each case offers an argument for whether or not the measure is justified.

Donald F. Kettl, *System Under Stress: Homeland Security and American Politics.* Washington, DC: CQ, 2004. Kettl broadly discusses the political difficulties of implementing homeland security measures. One of seven chapters focuses on the Patriot Act.

Richard C. Leone and Greg Anrig Jr., eds., *The War on Our Freedoms: Civil Liberties in an Age of Terrorism.* New York: PublicAffairs, 2003. This anthology features thirteen essays on civil liberties in the war on terrorism. Most emphasize the need for checks and balances to prevent the abuse of counterterrorism measures.

Michael W. Ritz, Ralph G. Hensley Jr., and James C. Whitmire, eds., *The Homeland Security Papers: Stemming the Tide of Terror.* Maxwell Air Force Base, AL: USAF Counterproliferation Center, February 2004. This collection of ten essays on homeland security, written from a military perspective, includes one essay focused on how the Patriot Act affects civil liberties.

Periodicals

John Berlau, "Money Laundering and Mission Creep," *Insight on the News,* January 5, 2004.

Vanessa Blum, "Pitching the Patriot Act," *Legal Times,* August 2, 2004.

Robyn E. Blumner, "If You Liked Patriot I, Don't Miss the Sequel," *St. Petersburg Times,* February 16, 2003.

Bob Dart, "Patriot Act Faces Opposition from the Left and Right," *San Diego Union-Tribune,* March 23, 2005.

Michael Duffy and Nancy Gibbs, "How Far Do We Want the FBI to Go?" *Time*, June 10, 2002.

Steve Friess, "Patriot Act Gets Mixed Reviews in Vegas," *Boston Globe*, November 8, 2003.

Kevin Galvin, "Rights and Wrongs," *Seattle Times*, December 6, 2001.

Michael Isikoff, "Show Me the Money," *Newsweek*, December 1, 2003.

Richard Lamm, "Terrorism and Immigration: We Need a Border," *Vital Speeches of the Day*, March 1, 2002.

Eric Lichtblau, "Administration Plans Defense of Terror Law," *New York Times*, August 19, 2003.

———, "U.S. Uses Terror Law to Pursue Crimes from Drugs to Swindling," *New York Times*, September 28, 2003.

Chuck McCutcheon, "Dispute Looms on Patriot Act Renewals," *Times-Picayune*, March 23, 2005.

Ann McFeatters and Karen MacPherson, "Patriot Act May See Revisions," *Pittsburgh Post-Gazette*, April 26, 2004.

Jim McGee, "An Intelligence Giant in the Making," *Washington Post*, November 4, 2001.

David Mehegan, "Literary Groups Decry Patriot Act as Invasion of Privacy," *Boston Globe*, May 16, 2003.

Robert O'Harrow, "Six Weeks in Autumn," *Washington Post*, October 27, 2002.

San Francisco Chronicle, "Privacy and Security; A Librarian's Dilemma," February 2, 2003.

Charlie Savage, "Civil-Liberties Issue in the Background," *Boston Globe*, October 4, 2004.

Sam Stanton and Emily Bazar, "Patriot Act's Broad Brush," *Sacramento Bee*, December 21, 2003.

Stuart Taylor Jr., "Rights, Liberties, and Security: Recalibrating the Balance After September 11," *Brookings Review*, Winter 2003.

Frank Viviano, "Organized Crime Said to Launder Billions for Terrorists," *San Francisco Chronicle*, September 23, 2001.

Fareed Zakaria, "The Answer? A Domestic CIA," *Newsweek*, May 27, 2002.

James D. Zirin, "Fearful Patriot Act?" *Washington Times*, October 22, 2004.

Internet Sources

American Civil Liberties Union, *Civil Liberties After 9/11: The ACLU Defends Freedom*. www. aclu.org/SafeandFree.Safeand Free.cfm?ID=108988&c=207.

———, "How the Anti-Terrorism Bill Allows for Detention of People Engaging in Innocent Associational Activity," October 23, 2001. www.aclu.org/National Security/NationalSecurity.cfm?ID=915 2&c=111.

———, *Insatiable Appetite: The Government's Demand for New and Unnecessary Powers After September 11*, April 2002. www.aclu.org/Files/OpenFile.cfm ?id=14799.

———, "List of Communities That Have Passed Resolutions." www.aclu.org/Safe andFree/.

———, "Section 215 FAQ," October 24, 2002. www.aclu.org/Privacy/Privacy.cfm ?ID=11054&c=130.

———, *Unpatriotic Acts: The FBI's Power to Rifle Through Your Records and Personal Belongings Without Telling You*. New York: ACLU, July 2003. www.aclu.org/ Files/OpenFile.cfm?id=13245.

American Library Association, "Resolution on the Patriot Act," January 29, 2003.

www.ala.org/Template.cfm?Section=ifre
solutions&Template=/ContentManage
ment/Cor.

John Ashcroft, letter to Senator Orrin Hatch,
January 28, 2004. www.cdt.org.

———, press conference, October 18, 2001.
www.usdoj.gov/archive/ag/speeches/
2001/agcrisisremarks10_18.htm.

———, "The Proven Tactics in the Fight
Against Crime," Washington, DC, September 15, 2003. www.usdoj.gov/archive/
ag/speeches/2003/091503nationalrestau
rant.htm.

———, remarks before the Federalist Society
National Convention, November 15, 2003.
www.lifeandliberty.gov/subs/speeches/
agspeechfeder.htm.

———, remarks before U.S. Mayors Conference, October 25, 2001. www.usdoj.gov/
archive/ag/speeches/2001/agcrisisremarks
10_25.htm.

———, speech before the American Enterprise Institute, August 19, 2003. www.aei.
org/publications/pubID.19040,filter.all/.

———, testimony before the House Committee on the Judiciary, September 24,
2001. www.usdoj.gov/archive/ag/testi
mony/2001/agcrisisremarks9_24.htm.

Bob Barr, testimony before the Senate Judiciary Committee, September 22, 2004.
http://judiciary.senate.gov/testimony.cf
m?id=1312&wit_id=2874.

George W. Bush, remarks at Kleinshans
Music Hall, Buffalo, NY, April 20, 2004.
www.whitehouse.gov/news/releases/
2004/04/20040420.

———, remarks before the FBI Academy,
Quantico, VA, September 10, 2003.
www.whitehouse.gov/news/releases/
2003/09/images/20030910_6_quantico
2=d-pm-0910-515h.html.

———, "President Signs Anti-Terrorism

Bill," October 26, 2001. www.white
house.gov/news/releases/2001/10/.

Center for Constitutional Rights, *The State
of Civil Liberties: One Year Later*, September 2002. www.ccr-ny.org.

Center for Democracy and Technology,
"Patriot Act Sunsets," May 7, 2004. www.
cdt.org/security/usapatriot/analysis.
shtml.

———, "What's Wrong with the Patriot Act
and How to Fix It." www.cdt.org/security/
usaptriot/brochure.pdf.

Nancy Chang, *The USA Patriot Act: What's
So Patriotic About Trampling the Bill of
Rights?* Center for Constitutional
Rights, November 2001. www.ccr-ny.
org/v2/reports/dos/USA_PATRIOT_
ACT.pdf.

Coalition in Defense of Freedom, "In
Defense of Freedom at a Time of Crisis,"
September 18, 2001. www.american
humanist.org/press/coalition.html.

Dan Collins, testimony before the Senate
Judiciary Committee, September 22,
2004. http://judiciary.senate.gov/testi
mony.cfm?id=1312.

James X. Dempsey, "Civil Liberties in a Time
of Crisis," *Human Rights*, Winter 2002.
www.abanet.org/irr/hr/winter02/demp
sey.html.

Dick Durbin, "Bipartisan Group of Senators
Unveil 'Safe Act,'" October 15, 2003.
http://durbin.senate.gov.

Electronic Frontier Foundation, "FOIA
Request to DOJ Concerning Pen-Trap
Surveillance," January 13, 2005. www.eff.
org/news/archives/2005_01.php.

Findlaw for Legal Professionals, *United
States v. United States District Court*,
407 U.S. 297 (1972). http://laws.findlaw.
com/us/407/297.html.

Alice Fisher, testimony before the Senate

Judiciary Committee, October 9, 2002. http://judiciary.senate.gov/testimony.cfm?id=495&wit_id=1249.

Patrick J. Fitzgerald, testimony before the Senate Judiciary Committee, October 21, 2003. http://judiciary.senate.gov/testimony. cfm?id=1439&wit_id=3936.

Alberto Gonzales, remarks before the National Association of Counties Legislative Conference, Washington, DC, March 7, 2005. www.usdoj.gov/ag/speeches/ 2005/ 03072005_naco.htm.

Patrick Leahy, statement on the passage of the Patriot Act, October 25, 2001. http:// leahy.senate.gov/issues/targetterror/.

———, Statement on the request for subpoenas in terrorism cases, Senate Judiciary Committee, June 22, 2004. http:// judiciary.senate.gov/print_member_ statement.cfm?id=1235&wit_id=2629.

Dahlia Lithwick and Julia Turner, "A Guide to the Patriot Act, Part 1," *Slate*, September 8, 2003. http://slate.msn.com/id/ 2087984/.

———, "A Guide to the Patriot Act, Part 2," *Slate*, September 10, 2003. http://slate. msn.com/id/2088106/.

———, "A Guide to the Patriot Act, Part 4," *Slate*, September 11, 2003. http://slate. msn.com/id/2088239/.

Heather MacDonald, "Straight Talk on Homeland Security," *City Journal*, vol. 13, no. 3, Summer 2003. www.city-journal. org/html/13_3_straight_talk.html.

Robert S. Mueller III, statement before the National Commission on Terrorist Attacks upon the United States, April 14, 2004. www.fbi.gov/congress/congress04/ mueller041404.htm.

Patriots to Restore Checks and Balances. www.checksbalances.org

John Podesta, "USA Patriot Act: The Good, the Bad, and the Sunset," *Human Rights*, Winter 2002. www.abanet.org/irr/hr/ winter02/podesta.html.

Pollingreport.com, "War on Terrorism."

Mark Reibling, "Uncuff the FBI," *Opinion-Journal*, June 4, 2002. www.opinion journal.com/editorial/feature.html.

Robin Rice, "The USA Patriot Act and American Libraries," *Information for Social Change*, Winter 2002/2003. www. libr.org/ISC/articles/16-Rice.html.

Ruth Rosen, "Could It Happen Again?" *San Francisco Chronicle*, May 12, 2003. www. commondreams.org/views03/0512-01.htm.

Matthew Rothschild, "The New McCarthyism," *Progressive*, January 2002. http:// secure.progressive.org/0901/roth0102. html.

Select Committee to Study Government Operations With Respect to Intelligence Activities, *Intelligence Activities and the Rights of Americans, Book II*, April 26, 1976. www.icdc.com/~paulwolf/cointel pro/churchfinalreport//ca.htm.

Jay Stanley and Barry Steinhardt, *Bigger Monster, Weaker Chains: The Growth of the American Surveillance Society*, New York: ACLU, January 2003. www.aclu.org/ Privacy/Privacy.cfm?ID=11572.

USA Patriot Act, H.R. 3162, October 24, 2001. www.findlaw.com.

U.S. Department of Justice, "Dispelling the Myths." Preserving Life & Liberty. www. lifeandliberty.gov/subs/u_myths.htm.

Jay Winik, "Security Before Liberty: Today's Curbs on Freedom Are Nothing Compared with Earlier Wars," *OpinionJournal*, October 23, 2001. www.opinion journal.com/editorial/feature.html.

Index

Picture Credits

Cover: Getty Images
AP Wide World Photos, 50, 54, 77
© Bernard Annebicque/CORBIS SYGMA, 48
© Bettmann/CORBIS, 44
© CORBIS, 10
Dennis Brack/Landov, 42
Gerald L. Nino/MAI/Landov, 53
Getty Images, 78
© Images.com/CORBIS, 9
© Jim Bourg/Reuters/CORBIS, 61
© Joe Skipper/Reuters/CORBIS, 26
Kevin Dietsch/UPI/Landov
© Les Stone/CORBIS, 51
Library of Congress, 47, 58
© Mark Wilson/Pool/Reuters/CORBIS, 74
Maury Aaseng, 29
Photos.com, 37
© Raiman Talaie/CORBIS, 73
© Reuters/CORBIS, 13, 14, 18, 23, 24, 57, 62, 69, 79
Roger L. Wollenberg/UPI/Landov, 39
© Roger Ressmeyer/CORBIS, 65
Sherburne County Sheriff's Office Handout/Reuters/Landov, 32

About the Author

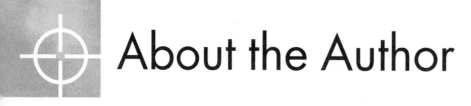

James D. Torr is a freelance writer and editor who has worked on a variety of publications for Greenhaven Press and Lucent Books.